'A wonderful and long-overdue boo[...] [...]ble that shows

difference through God's lens. The way the stories are told is upbeat and

positive, showing children with any sort of additional need that they are part of

God's story too. There's no pity, no patronising, just the overriding theme that

people in the Bible who had difficulties, disadvantages and disabilities also

had a part to play in God's big and amazing adventure.'

Kay Morgan-Gurr, Chair of Children Matter and Co-founder of the

Additional Needs Alliance

'A witty, warm and wise book that is long overdue.

A book to help all children (and their grown-ups) know they are loved

and treasured, just the way they are!'

Revd Kate Bottley, Anglican Priest in the Diocese of Southwell and Nottingham

KRISH AND MIRIAM KANDIAH
ILLUSTRATED BY ANDY GRAY

WHISTLESTOP TALES

AROUND THE BIBLE WITH 10 EXTRAORDINARY CHILDREN

First published in Great Britain in 2022 by Hodder & Stoughton
An Hachette UK Company

This paperback edition first published 2023

1

Paperback ISBN 978 1 399 80132 4
ebook ISBN 978 1 399 80131 7

Typeset by Andy S. Gray, Onegraydot Ltd.

Printed and bound in Great Britain by Clays Ltd, Elcograf S.p.A.

Hodder & Stoughton policy is to use papers that are natural, renewable
and recyclable products and made from wood grown in sustainable forests.
The logging and manufacturing processes are expected to conform to the
environmental regulations of the country of origin.

Hodder & Stoughton Ltd
Carmelite House
50 Victoria Embankment
London EC4Y 0DZ

www.hodderfaithyoungexplorers.co.uk

This book is dedicated to all
our extraordinary children,
foster children, nephews, nieces,
neighbours and god-children.
At least ten of you will spot
yourselves in the pages of this
book. Thank you for inspiring us.

CONTENTS

Dear friend,

When I was your age I often felt that I didn't really fit in, and not just because I was the only boy in my class who wasn't white. I also happened to be the shortest boy in my class, which meant that everyone looked down at me all the time. Sometimes it made me feel lonely and worthless.

I couldn't do anything about the colour of my skin, but perhaps I could do something about my height — or lack of it. I tried dangling from the top of the doorframe every evening to stretch myself. I tried eating lots of spinach and extra vitamins. I tried standing on tiptoes and spiking my hair up. Even then I was still shorter than everyone else I knew.

Each week at church I was told stories of people in the Bible who got miraculously healed, so I began to pray that God would make me taller. When he didn't answer those prayers, I began to wonder if he even cared.

Then I made a discovery that really helped me. It turns out there are quite a lot of heroes of the Bible who never got miraculously healed. Some of them were looked down on too. Some of them felt worthless. But God took the very things that were different about them, and did something incredible.

The children in my life and family often remind me of these stories. Some of them have what school might call 'additional needs', or 'special needs', or 'learning differences'. Some of them have physical disabilities. All of them worry from time to time about being or looking or feeling different. It turns out God has wonderful plans for their lives too.

If, like me, you have ever felt like you didn't fit in, or like many children, worry about the things that make you different, I hope the tales my wife Miriam and I have written will help you too. They might not be quite like the Bible tells them, but we hope you will discover through them the amazing truth that God loves you and wants to fit you, yes you, with your own wonderfully unique differences, into his global adventure.

Your friend,

Krish

SADIE'S STORY

This is Sadie. You can see she has the most amazing smile. She also has an amazing story.

When she was born, Sadie weighed less than a bag of apples. She couldn't breathe without a machine. She needed feeding through a plastic tube. Both Sadie and her twin brother had to fight to survive.

Sadie had another tool in her survival kit — that amazing smile. It took her to places her legs wouldn't take her. Even though she struggled to walk, she could always smile her way into people's hearts. Our family fell in love with her during the years she lived with us, and still burst with pride whenever we think about her skipping down the hill to school with her new adoptive family.

We wish Sadie could meet Jacob who appears in the first book of the Bible. He was another twin with a complicated family story who ended up walking differently through the world too.

3

JACOB

THE TALE OF THE BROTHER WHO LEARNED TO WALK DIFFERENTLY THROUGH THE WORLD

In the middle of the river, in the middle of the night, in the middle of nowhere, a man found himself standing up to his middle in cold, murky water. Slimy riverweed stuck to his wet clothes. Swampy underwater creatures brushed past his bare legs. Large, ugly flies hovered around his ears, buzzing in excitement at their unexpected visitor.

But something much worse was bothering the man. Perhaps you know what it's like to be in such terrible trouble, there is nobody left to talk to but yourself. Well, that was how this man in the middle of this Middle Eastern river was feeling.

'Jacob, you idiot,' he shouted at himself as his eyes darted from one riverbank to the other and back again. 'You've gone and done it this time.

You can't go left. You can't go right.
What are you going to do now?'

To his left was darkness, and Jacob knew that somewhere in that darkness was someone he never, ever, *ever* wanted to see ever, ever again.

'You can't risk going that way,' Jacob said – to himself again. 'You'll end up back at your stinky Uncle Laban's farm – working day and night for next to nothing like before. That's if he doesn't kill you first.'

Jacob had never met anyone quite as stinky as stinky Uncle Laban. For a start he stank of smelly sheep, and hadn't had a bath for as long as anyone could remember. He was also stinking rich, and, like many stinking rich people, refused to pay anyone their proper wages. And on top of that he caused such a stink at Jacob's wedding that he made Jacob's life a misery for 14 long years. I mean, what sort of person sneakily swaps the bride for her sister so you marry the wrong girl?

Jacob turned and looked at the opposite bank. There was darkness that way too. And somewhere in it was everything he had just stolen from Uncle Laban and sent across the river ahead of him. This included:

2,739 sheep and goats,

423 cows and bulls,

56 grown-up camels,

12 baby camels,

35 donkeys,

3 ridiculously expensive family heirlooms,

60 company staff,

plus 12 children. And one more on the way.

'But what's the use of being rich if you can't enjoy it?' the man waist-deep in the river moaned out loud to himself, wishing he was brave enough to join them on the opposite bank.

'You can't risk going that way either, Jacob. There's an army on its way to capture you dead or alive. Preferably dead.'

If Jacob wasn't already freezing from standing in cold water in the middle of the night, he might have felt his body shudder. If he'd had hairs on his strangely smooth arms, they would have stood up on end. If his hands weren't already dripping wet, he would have felt his palms begin to sweat. But Jacob didn't need reminding of just how scared he was. He had spent years hiding from the army that was out to get him, knowing that the moment he crossed the river, he would be signing his own death certificate.

You see, long before Jacob had run away with stinky Uncle Laban's family fortunes, he had run away with someone else's family fortunes. That someone else happened to be Esau. And Esau happened to be his twin brother.

The twin brother who had his own army.

The twin brother who never missed a target.

The twin brother who liked to hunt
his victims down, skin them, boil
them in a pan and
eat them for supper.

Jacob had
been born on the
wrong side of
Esau. They came
into the world
fighting, grew
up fighting and fought as their
father lay dying. They would have carried on fighting, too, if
Jacob hadn't sneakily taken everything that belonged to Esau,
and if Esau hadn't threatened
to take revenge, hunt him
down with his army and
kill him.

Do you have brothers and sisters who annoy you sometimes? Perhaps you decide to get your own back now and then. Maybe you unplug their devices so they don't charge up. Or leave banana skins in their coat pockets so they smell. Whatever you've done to them, I really hope they don't practise slaughtering bears, lions and wolves, so they can try to get you back like Esau. And I really hope you don't need to run away to a whole different country to escape like Jacob.

With furious twin brother Esau and his army on one side of the river and furious Uncle Laban with his stinky bad mood on the other, Jacob was trapped. That was why he was standing in the middle of the river in the middle of nowhere in the middle of the night not daring to go in either direction and talking to himself.

'You're done for, Jacob. You'll never see the light of day again. Things can't get any worse.'

That's when things got a whole lot worse.

SPLASH! Suddenly a shadowy figure leapt into the water and ran towards him.

THWACK! The mysterious figure collided hard with Jacob in the middle of the river.

GRAB! The stranger wrapped his arms around Jacob.

SQUEEZE! Jacob could hardly breathe. His heart was pounding, and sweat poured down his face, as he tried to prise those arms off him before they made his insides explode in all directions.

But no matter how much Jacob wriggled, pulled, pushed, shoved or manoeuvred he couldn't shake his attacker. Nor could he shake the feeling that he had met this stranger somewhere before.

'Esau?' Jacob spluttered. 'Is that you? I'm sorry I cheated you and ran away with your family fortunes. Please forgive me!'

There was no reply. Jacob yanked at the arms tightening around his chest. They weren't as hairy as Esau's. And besides,

Esau wasn't the sort to grab you and wrestle you. He was the sort who stalked you and threw spears at you when you least expected it. You know what? It wasn't Esau at all!

'Uncle Laban?' Jacob tried. 'Is that you?

I'm sorry I cheated you and ran away with the family
fortunes. Please forgive me!'

Jacob twisted to get a glimpse of the man's face. It may have
been dark, but he could see no wrinkles around his eyes. He
could see teeth but they didn't seem rotten and crooked. And
the man certainly didn't smell like sheep dung. You know what?
It wasn't stinky Uncle Laban at all!

Jacob's body ached. He'd been fighting his attacker for what felt like hours. He'd tried all the wrestling moves he knew:

**the backbreaker,
the facebuster,**

**the sideslammer,
the powerbomb,**

**the
elbowjab,**

even the naughty-kneeknocker.

But no matter how hard he tried, he just couldn't beat this stranger.

Jacob's brain ached too. Who was this attacker? Was there someone else he'd annoyed by his sneaking and cheating and tricking?

Meanwhile the stranger continued to fix his hold. Jacob gritted his teeth, snarled and pushed back again. Surely the assailant had to tire eventually. Nobody could hold on forever. Right?

Another hour went past. And another. Jacob's body ached even more. Jacob's brain ached even more.

He summoned up the last of his strength and shoved the stranger as hard as he could.

OUCH! It was Jacob who suddenly screamed out in pain.

EEEEEEHH! The top of his leg felt like it was burning. And why couldn't he feel his toes?

AAAH! Tears rolled down his cheeks as he shifted his weight to his other leg, and used his last bit of strength to put the stranger into what he hoped was a death grip.

Finally the attacker spoke. 'Let me go!'

Jacob racked his tired brains. Where had he heard that voice before?

His mind shot back to a night 20 years earlier when he had first run away from Esau. He had been exhausted from spending the whole day running, but once darkness had fallen he also became terrified. Jacob was alone for the first time in his life and he was convinced he was going to die. He lay down on a rock in the desert and waited to be eaten by wild animals. But when he closed his eyes, something lit up – a team of angels watching over him and busily going back and forth between Jacob in the desert and God in heaven. In his fear he clearly heard God say to him: 'Jacob, I am with you. I will not let you go.'

'Let me go!' the stranger called out again.

That voice! IT WAS GOD'S VOICE!

Rays of sunshine suddenly began to stream down towards the river. As they bounced back off the water, the lurking fish darted into the shadows. The flies and other scary night creatures vanished into their daytime hideaways. There was a moment of peace as dawn broke over the Middle East. Jacob, who was quite surprised to find himself still alive, felt the warmth of the sunlight on his exhausted, aching, broken body.

'I can't let you go,' Jacob said. 'Please stay with me. I need your help!'

'Really?' asked the stranger. 'Who are you, anyway?'

Jacob hung his head and sighed. 'Who am I? I'm an idiot. I'm the sort of person who tricks their own father, cheats their own brother and swindles their own uncle.

(Although my uncle did swindle me first, so he sort of deserved it.) I'm the sort of person who forgets to trust God. I'm a thief and a runaway. (Well, I *was* a runaway – now I don't think I'll ever run again.) I'm a failure.'

The stranger handed Jacob a strong stick to lean on and smiled.

'You're not a failure. In fact I declare you the winner of our wrestling match. And as the first person in history to wrestle with God – *and win* – millions of people will follow in your footsteps.'

'I won?' Jacob repeated, dragging his useless leg carefully out of the river.

'Millions of people?' he wondered, as the stranger disappeared.

'Follow in my footsteps?'

Jacob clambered up the bank and hobbled off in the middle of the day, in the middle of the dusty road, in the middle of somewhere in the Middle East.

Far away on that dusty road Jacob could see an army of 400 men marching towards him with shields and spears. Leading the way was his brother Esau. With every limping step Jacob took, he was reminded of his own weakness and of God's strength. If millions of people were going to follow in his footsteps, he would first need to get out of this trouble. He couldn't run any more, and he couldn't fight any longer. He wondered what options were left.

Jacob

CRASH! Jacob watched as Esau threw down his shield and spear and began running. Perhaps it was the signal to attack.

THWACK! Esau collided with his brother in the middle of the road.

GRAB! Esau wrapped his hairy arms around his brother.

SQUEEZE! For the second time that day Jacob could hardly breathe.

Finally he got the words out that had been trapped inside him for 20 years.

'**I'm sorry, Esau.** You can have everything. I'll be your servant for as long as I live.'

Jacob didn't think that would be many more minutes.

With that Esau squeezed Jacob even tighter. It wasn't an attack, but an **embrace**.

Tears rolled down Esau's face as he showered kisses on his long-lost brother. Jacob may have stolen his family fortunes and run away to a far-off country, but now he was back!

All was forgiven.

'I'm sorry about your leg,' Esau said, a little while later, as they slowly walked home arm in arm. Following closely behind them were:

2,739 sheep and goats,
423 cows and bulls,
56 grown-up camels,
12 baby camels,
35 donkeys,
3 ridiculously expensive family heirlooms,
60 company staff,
12 children,
and 1 more on the way.
Oh, and 400 armed and confused soldiers.

'I'm sorry too,' said Jacob, who still could hardly believe that his brother had been waiting all those years, longing for him to return. If only he'd realised sooner. 'I'm sorry for so many things. But I'm not sorry about my leg. From now on I'm going to walk differently through the world and I will trust God every step of the way.'

After Jacob found the forgiveness of God and his brother at long last, he lost a couple of important things. First he lost one of his children, but found him again years later. Then he lost all his food supplies, but found some more in a country far away. But Jacob never lost his trust in God. Millions of people around the world have followed in his footsteps. You can read Jacob's story for yourself in Genesis 32–50.

EVIE'S STORY

This is Evie. If she could talk to you right now you might hear her words getting muddled. She often says funny things by accident — like 'hodgeheg' or 'paintfacing' or 'me-rote control'.

But just because Evie doesn't always have the right words, it doesn't mean she has no voice. If she could sing to you right now you would hear that God has given her an amazing talent. Even I don't have the words to describe how beautiful she sounds when she sings.

We'd love Evie to meet Moses, a boy from ancient Egypt who also felt embarrassed about the way he spoke. When Moses discovered that God wanted to use his voice for something very important, he had a big decision to make.

MOSES

THE TALE OF THE PRINCE WHO WAS LOST FOR WORDS

Cup of coffee. Cup of coffee. Cup of coffee.

Say that slowly out loud. Now try to say it faster. How fast can you say it without saying Cuff of Coppee?

Perhaps you know some other tongue twisters. It can be quite funny when your mouth won't do what you want it to do, and you end up saying nonsense.

All people find some words tricky, but some people find all words tricky. If you know what that's like, you know that it doesn't seem funny at all. It can make you want to run away and hide.

Like Moses.

When Moses was born, his mum had to keep him a secret because he was a Hebrew baby boy and Pharaoh had ordered

that all Hebrew baby boys
should be killed. Every time
baby Moses made a sound his
mother shushed him and covered
his mouth. Baby Moses had to be
quiet. His life depended on it.

  After a while Moses' mother
couldn't keep her baby a secret any longer. So
she put him in a watertight basket and placed him in the river,
hoping someone would rescue him. She never expected that
someone to be from Pharaoh's family. The Princess adopted
Moses to protect him, but she had to be careful. She didn't
want Pharaoh hearing him
speak Egyptian with a
Hebrew accent. The
Princess shushed
him. Moses had to
be quiet. His life
depended on it.

Many years later Moses saw one of Pharaoh's soldiers beat up a Hebrew slave who had done nothing wrong. Moses was angry. He could easily have stopped the fight with a threat to report back to the Princess. But he didn't have the words. So he let his fists do the talking. When Pharaoh found out that Moses had lost his temper, he issued a death warrant. That would shush him for good. Moses quietly ran away. His life depended on it.

Moses ran and ran. He ran for hours. The hours turned into days and the days turned into weeks. Moses ran all the way

across Egypt, over the border and half way across Saudi Arabia. There he slumped down beside a well. Helping himself to a long cool drink, he wondered how much further he should run to be far enough away from Pharaoh and his death threats.

As Moses wondered, seven women arrived closely followed by a lot of very thirsty sheep. One by one the women dropped their watertight baskets into the well, heaved them out again, and tipped the water into troughs. Then they went back for more. They were strong and they were smiling. But Moses could see it was going to take them all afternoon to fill the troughs with enough water for so many sheep.

Moses couldn't help but get a huge lump in his throat as he watched the women. They reminded him of how his Hebrew mother had once lowered him in a basket into the river. They reminded him of how his Egyptian mother had pulled that basket out of the water. Those strong, brave women had saved his life. Now he would never see anyone from his family ever again. He shuddered at the thought of what Pharaoh might do to them.

As Moses fought back tears, a gang of sweaty farmers arrived at the well in a really bad mood. They kicked the sheep away from the troughs and laughed in the women's faces. Then they snatched the baskets, drank the water that was left in them, and tossed them between each other over the women's heads. The women tried to walk away but the farmers just blocked their path and shouted at them. Moses didn't understand a word they were saying, but he knew it wasn't polite. His fists curled themselves into weapons.

He wanted to bash those farmers to bits and mash them into a pile of sheep dung.

He wanted to grab those farmers by the ankles and drop them head first into the deep well.

He wanted to chase them across the Saudi Arabian desert and hand them over to Pharaoh.

Moses glanced at the women and remembered his two mothers again. He slowly uncurled his fists, pulled up his sleeves and walked right into the middle of the gang of sweaty farmers. He didn't walk away again until he had every single one of the women's baskets hooked over his arm. Then, without saying a single word, he filled those baskets up over and over and over again. Before long every single sheep had more than enough to drink.

The farmers couldn't believe their eyes. Who was this strong, silent, strange man? And what was he doing helping women? No Saudi Arabian men at that time would have been seen dead doing that. In fact, no Saudi Arabian men at that time would have been seen dead even watching another man do that. Off they ran as fast as they could and were never seen at that well ever again.

The women couldn't believe their eyes either. Those sweaty farmers had been bullying them for weeks. Now they were gone for good. Who was this brave,

kind stranger who had scared them away without raising a fist or even saying a word? The women took him straight home for dinner to find out. There he stayed. Moses settled down to spend the rest of his life watching the women's sheep as they wandered in the deserted desert fields. He never needed to speak to anyone again!

Or so he thought.

Years went by and Moses had almost forgotten that he was still a fugitive from Pharaoh.

But one day as he sat quietly watching the sheep, Moses heard something that made it all come racing back.

'Moses!' came the voice from nowhere.

Moses jumped up and looked around. His heart raced. He couldn't see anyone – just a ball of tumbleweed skimming across the sand and a bush that had sparked into flame in the heat of the day. Nothing unusual for a hot desert afternoon.

Perhaps it was just his imagination playing tricks on him.

'Moses!' said the voice again.

Moses looked around again. He still couldn't see anyone.

Although he did look twice at that bush.

Usually shrubbery that caught fire in the desert sun burned up immediately. One minute it would be there. The next it would have disappeared, leaving behind a small pile of ash. This bush just kept burning. But although that was surprising, Moses was far more shocked at the strange voice calling out his name in the middle of nowhere where nobody knew him. It had been years since anyone had bothered trying to have a conversation with him.

'Moses! Moses!'

The voice was gentle but strong. Kind but serious. Frightening but also welcoming. Moses could feel his heart burning in his chest.

'Here I am!'

Moses whispered. He wasn't sure what else to say. He'd hardly said anything for years, and certainly not to a fiery bush.

Except it wasn't a fiery bush he was talking to.

It was God himself.

MOSES!

MOSES!

Moses had no doubt about it. The voice was so powerful, even stars and galaxies would have done what they were told.

God wasn't talking to stars and galaxies. He was talking to him, the fugitive from Pharaoh.

'Moses, take off your shoes.'

Moses did as he was told. He didn't even notice that the hot desert sand *wasn't* scorching his feet. He was far too busy being *terrified*. He never imagined he would meet God in a desert in Saudi Arabia. He thought he was safely hidden away.

There was clearly nowhere left to hide.

So Moses did what everyone does when they don't want to be seen but there's nowhere to hide: he covered his eyes. But his hands could no more hide him, than the burning leaves of the bush could hide the majesty of God. Besides, Moses should probably have chosen to cover his ears instead, because he didn't like what he heard next *at all* !

'Moses!' said God's voice from the bush. 'Go back to Egypt and tell Pharaoh to let my people go. I won't let them be tormented any more.'

'who, me ?!'

Moses' head was spinning. How could he find the words to explain to God all the reasons why this was such a terrible idea? Moses wasn't the right man for the job at all. He was the **opposite** of the right man. He could just imagine what a job application form would have looked like.

First name: Moses.

Family name: Depends which family you're talking about.

Nationality: Hmmmm. Not sure.

How well can you speak Egyptian?

Err, badly.

How well can you speak Hebrew?

Errrrrrrmmmm. Worse than badly.

Do you have any work experience?

I'm good at watching sheep eat grass.

Do you have a Criminal Record?

Does murder count?

Can you start tomorrow? Well, I currently live a week's walk away . . . So . . . No!

'No, God!' Moses said.

Moses clapped his hand over his mouth. Had he really just said, 'No' to God? But going back to Egypt was impossible. His arms dropped to his side, as he remembered the terrible thing he had done. He should never have lost his temper with Pharaoh' soldier.

'No, God! You have the wrong person.'

Moses knew he wasn't making any sense at all. God didn't make mistakes.

'No, God! Pharaoh won't listen to me.'

True, but even Moses knew it was no reason to refuse to do what God asked.

'No, God! I can't even speak properly. Send someone else.'

For someone who couldn't speak properly, Moses was doing a pretty good job at arguing, don't you think?

When Moses had finished arguing, he waited for God's fire to engulf him and reduce him to a pile of ash in the desert. He knew he deserved it.

That's when God spoke the words that would change Moses' life.

'DON'T BE AFRAID. I WILL BE WITH YOU.'

Moses had spent his whole life being afraid. He had picked up the fear from his Hebrew mother before he was even born. He had learned fear from his Egyptian mother – anyone who lived in Pharaoh's palace feared daily for their lives. Moses had always felt scared and alone and useless. He couldn't speak properly. He didn't fit in and had no idea what his purpose was in life. He thought God had forgotten about him, just like he seemed to have forgotten the Hebrew people Pharaoh was tormenting.

But God never forgets about anyone. Even if they forget about him. God certainly never forgets about those who are suffering.

'Moses, go and tell Pharaoh to let my people go.'

Moses had no arguments left. So he got up, walked all the way back to Egypt and did what God had told him to do.

Delivering a message for God is never easy. Moses knew it was going to be difficult, but he never imagined just how extremely difficult it would turn out to be.

There were gruesome plagues.
And armies on chariots.
And killer rivers.

And even fiery serpents.
God helped Moses and
kept him safe every time.

'Don't
be afraid. I
will be with
you,' he said.

Many, many, many years later Moses woke up early and quietly wandered off into the Saudi Arabian desert. This time there was no fiery bush, but Moses knew by now that God was always with him.

He looked out across the sandy panorama – hundreds and hundreds of tents were pitched there. One of them belonged to his brother – he always helped him when his words got stuck. Another belonged to his sister – she had a wonderful talent for singing. The rest of the tents were filled with his enormous Hebrew family – all those he had helped to rescue from Egypt. God had led them right back to where it had all started.

But it wasn't the end of the story. Moses was waiting for God's voice to speak to him again and tell him where to lead the people to next on their adventure.

For someone who found it hard to speak, Moses ended up saying a lot: five whole books of the Bible and one psalm are attributed to Moses. That's more than anyone else by a very long way. Moses' encounter with God in the fiery bush is recorded in Exodus 3 and 4, but there's plenty more to discover about him in the Bible, along with other surprising people God used to speak on his behalf.

CHARLIE'S STORY

This is Charlie. Charlie is 8. He loves football, burgers and video games and isn't very good at sitting still. Sometimes children laugh at Charlie when he's struggling at school. Most days the teachers take him into the corridor or outside to work where nobody can distract him. Often that makes the bullying worse. Charlie's family can't help him because they have a lot of problems of their own. So he lives with us while they sort them out.

Charlie has just made a few friends at

church and at the football club who realise that life is hard for him and go out of their way to be kind. Perhaps Rahab would have been a friend to charlie too. She understood what it was like to feel like an outsider.

We like to imagine charlie meeting Rahab. We think they'd have lots to talk about. Perhaps he could tell her about video games and football. Perhaps she could tell him her story of how God helped her when she felt like an outsider, and how she was welcomed into a new family.

RAHAB

THE TALE OF THE GIRL WHOSE WORLD CAME CRASHING DOWN

Rahab did **NOT** like going to school. It wasn't because she never won any races on sports day, although she never did. It wasn't because the school dinners were revolting,

even though they made her sick. It definitely wasn't because she wasn't intelligent, because she was, in fact, surprisingly smart.

The reason

Rahab did **NOT** like school was because of the bullying. From the moment she arrived to the moment

she got home she

was teased, picked on, pushed around, and laughed at. The other children pulled her hair, called her names, chased her around, tripped her over and then did it all again. And again.

Rahab did what you are supposed to do with bullies: she walked away, she acted brave, she stood up to them and she told the teachers. But back in Rahab's school this didn't help one little bit. You see the teachers were the worst bullies of the lot! Instead of helping Rahab, they joined in making her life miserable. They pulled her hair, called her names, chased her around, tripped her over and then did it all again. And again. *Can you imagine?! The teachers!!*

Rahab lived in Jericho over three thousand years ago, long before children were taught reading and writing and being respectful at school. The children in Rahab's class were taught their ABCs: arguing, bullying and cheating. Each class of children was supposed to become meaner and nastier than the one before. In that way, the town could uphold its reputation for being the meanest, nastiest place in the world.

In Jericho nobody said polite things like 'please' or 'thank you' or 'you're welcome' – they said mean and nasty things like 'I want!' and 'Go away!' and 'Shut up!'

In Jericho, nobody knocked on your door and popped in for a cup of tea. Instead mean and nasty people would just barge right into your house and help themselves to anything they wanted.

In Jericho, people didn't name their children nice things with nice meanings, but mean and nasty things like *Useless* and *Smelly* and, in Rahab's case, *Fat*.

There was even a mean and nasty sign outside Jericho that said: **'KEEP OUT – WE MEAN IT'**. The sign was pinned to a huge wall that was 4 metres tall and 2 metres thick and patrolled by mean and nasty guards with vicious dogs.

Rahab wasn't very good at being mean and nasty. That's why her school report looked like this:

Arguing Grade: **FAIL**

Comment: Rahab is bad at being bad.

Bullying Grade: **FAIL**

Comment: Rahab must learn to pick on people smaller than she is.

Cheating Grade: **FAIL**

Comment: Honestly a terrible student. Rahab can't lie to save her life.

If Rahab had known there was a God who cared about people who were being bullied, she might have realised she wasn't a fat, worthless, stupid nobody like everyone said. But Rahab, like everyone else in Jericho, didn't know much about God. The only time he was ever mentioned was when a small camp of Israelite refugees made the headlines.

'Apparently they somehow escaped from Pharaoh's evil clutches,' thieves whispered as they stole from one another in Jericho's marketplace. 'They claim God helped them.'

'Did you hear about the tsunami that wiped out the entire Egyptian cavalry and saved the refugees' lives?' the Jericho

criminals mumbled as they kicked passers-by for no reason.

'Now God has helped them get rid of King Sihon the Spiteful!' muttered the murderers as they compared hit lists on the park bench. 'This God has got to go.'

Soon everyone in Jericho was talking about the fearsome, unstoppable God who seemed to be helping the small camp of Israelite refugees. But everyone said Jericho didn't need God. Jericho had its strong walls instead. And just to make sure, they also had their invincible neighbour: King Og, the Giant Ogre of Bashan. The Israelites would have to go past him to get to them. And nobody got past King Og, the Giant Ogre of Bashan.

Finally Rahab finished school and went out to find a job so she could earn money to help look after her brothers and sisters. But nobody would hire her. They all took one look at her and her FAIL grades and shook their heads with a laugh. Eventually Rahab had no other choice but to offer her services to the world's worst hotel.

The world's worst hotel on the edge of Jericho was not the sort of place you would ever want to visit. There were cockroaches in the kitchen, bed bugs crawling in the sheets and black furry mould growing on the cold, damp, stone walls.

Draughts whistled through the bars in the windows and the sticky grime on the staircases made guests slip and fall head over heels from top to bottom.

The smell from the toilet at the world's worst hotel was so bad you could taste it – even when you were eating your dinner, which, if you were lucky, might be a piece of stale bread and a bowl of dirty dishwater they called the super soup surprise.

If you dared go to bed at night in the world's worst hotel you would quickly discover you weren't alone. You see, there were no locks on the doors to stop mean and nasty strangers from bursting in in the middle of the night and helping themselves to whatever they fancied.

Working at the world's worst hotel turned out to be even worse than being at school. The bullying got meaner and meaner until Rahab was convinced there wasn't a shred of kindness or hope left in the entire city. She began to think about leaving, but there had been some bad news. It spread around the city like wildfire:

'King Og, the Giant Ogre of Bashan has been defeated!'

Everybody suddenly became petrified of the Israelite refugees who were making their way towards Jericho. When they were scared, the people of Jericho seemed to get even worse. The thieves did more thieving. The bullies did more bullying. The vandals did more vandalising. The murderers did more murdering.

That evening, as Rahab lay shivering in the bed she was sharing with far too many biting bedbugs and other creepy creatures, there was a soft knock on the front door.

A knock on the door?

A KNOCK ON THE DOOR?!

People in the city of Jericho didn't knock on the door! They barged right in. What was going on?

Rahab pulled the blanket around her shoulders, climbed out of bed and went downstairs. She opened the door to find two strange men standing on her doorstep.

'Can we have a bed for the night, please?' they asked at the same time.

Please?

PLEASE?!

People in the city of Jericho didn't say please. They said *'I WANT'*. Who were these men?

Rahab ushered the strangers in and took them upstairs to an empty room.

'Thank you,' they said in unison.

Thank you?

THANK YOU?!

This was very suspicious.

'Right, you two,' she said putting her hands on her hips and trying to sound as mean and nasty as she had been taught. 'Who are you? And where are you from? Do the authorities know you are here? How did you get past the city walls? What are you doing in Jericho?'

'I'm sorry if we've upset you,' one of the men replied. 'We arrived at the city gates this afternoon just in time to help the farmers with their deliveries. We are here for a few days to check out the city. We are Israelites'

'Yes, just Israelites,' the other man added nervously, 'just checking out the city.'

Rahab gasped. Israelites! Surely not! She knew she should lock them in and call the authorities immediately. If only the doors had locks.

'Tell me everything!' Rahab said, trying to buy herself some thinking time.

The two men began to tell their story.

'When we were your age, we lived in a country far away called Egypt. Pharaoh was in charge and he did not like our people. He was a terrible bully.'

'A terrible bully,' the second man echoed with a shudder.

'He beat the men, scared the women, forced children to work and even killed babies. We cried out to God to save us, but things got worse and worse.'

'And worse again. And then even worse than that.'

Rahab saw tears well up in the two men's eyes, and felt her own begin to prickle. She knew a bit about bullying and having no hope.

'Eventually, just when we thought we couldn't take it any more, we heard that God had a plan to rescue us. We packed our bags, painted a secret sign in our windows – a stripe of red blood, and waited. It was the most dreadful night of our lives.'

'The most dreadful. Yes. But also the most wonderful,' the second man added.

As the two men explained how God had punished Pharaoh and the mean and nasty Egyptians, Rahab began to understand why everyone in Jericho was petrified of him. But the men weren't scared of God. They told Rahab how God had not only rescued them out of the difficult situation, but had promised to get them safely to a new land where they could live in peace.

The more Rahab listened, the more she liked the sound of this Promised Land. It seemed like the world's best hotel. There was going to be space for everyone whatever they looked like and wherever they came from. There was to be no bullying or stealing or cheating. The menu would include fresh milk and sweet honey. And the children were to be taught kindness and how to be welcoming, just like their God.

'I wish I could live in a place like that,' Rahab sighed. 'Do you think …?'

Suddenly her thoughts were interrupted. Rahab could hear the authorities heading up the street. Any minute they would barge into the hotel and do something mean and nasty to her guests. How could she stop them?

'Hand over the spies!' shouted the angry crowd as they burst through the door.

'Spies ?!' Rahab said, opening her eyes as wide as she could. 'Spies? What spies?!'

Rahab thought about all her teachers and what they had said about her not being able to lie to save her life. Well now, she needed to tell a big, juicy lie to save the lives of the two men she had just hidden upstairs. She took a deep breath.

'If you mean the two hotel guests that arrived today ... err ... you missed them .... They've checked out already.'

The crowd looked angry. Some of them tried to push past her to get up the stairs. But she refused to move.

'They went that way!' Rahab added quickly and pointed a rather shaky finger in the opposite direction.

To her great surprise, everyone believed her and ran off to look for them.

There was no time to lose. The angry mob would be back just as soon as they realised they had been fooled by the girl who had once failed all her lying exams. Rahab rushed upstairs to fetch the two Israelite spies and a long rope. She tied one end tightly around her waist, threw the other out of the window and pushed her new friends towards the only escape route.

'Come with us, Rahab,' one of the men said as he began to climb out of the window. 'Quick – before that mean and nasty crowd gets back.'

Rahab wanted to go but she doubted she would fit through the window. Besides she would only slow the spies down. And she didn't want to leave her brothers and sisters behind. If only there was another way.

'Thank you, Rahab.' The second man lowered himself carefully down on the rope. 'One day we will welcome you to our home, just like you welcomed us to yours.'

Rahab wanted to believe him, but something was bothering her.

'God has to destroy this city,' she thought. 'It's the only way to stop the meanness and nastiness. And I deserve to be wiped out too. I'm nothing but a big fat liar from the world's worst hotel.'

As two shadowy figures ran away from Jericho in the middle of the night, Rahab heard their voices calling up to her.

'Rahab! You can trust our God. He won't let you down. Put a red stripe in your window. You and your family will be saved.'

A couple of weeks later Rahab finished her shopping and was heading back to the world's worst hotel with the heavy bags. All around her she could hear people laughing at the little army of Israelite refugees that that were now camping right outside Jericho's walls.

'Look at that pathetic army just sitting there doing nothing! They haven't even got proper weapons.'

'It's like they expect us to join in peace talks! What a joke!'

'If those weaklings could break down our walls, they would have done it by now.'

'They can't even march around the city more than once a day without sitting down to catch their breath.'

By the seventh day, the people of Jericho had decided God was just something the Israelites had made up to try and scare them. So they all went back to life as normal, which of course meant being as mean and nasty as possible.

Rahab watched the Israelite soldiers marching around the city from her window where a red cord she had found made a stripe down one side. She was nervous of leaving behind the only life she had ever known, but something inside her made her want to believe that it could all be so different. Maybe there were people out there who could be kind and welcoming; people who didn't see her just as a target to be bullied, but a life worth saving.

As she stood and watched, the army marched around the city, this time not just once, but seven times. Loud horn blasts echoed around Jericho. Dust began to engulf the city. The foundations started to tremble. Some of the frightened people of Jericho rushed to the massive walls around the city hoping

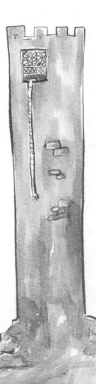

they would save them. They were wrong. There is never any barrier that God cannot overcome. The great walls of Jericho began to crumble and with an almighty crash tumbled to the ground.

The whole city had been turned into a pile of rubble. Only one window remained in place: the one with a red cord painting a stripe down one side.

The one where Rahab was waiting with her brothers and sisters.

Many years later, a little boy sat on Rahab's lap. It was his favourite place to curl up in the evening. And his favourite story was the one that ended with the great walls of Jericho crashing down.

'What happened next?' the boy asked this time.

Rahab smiled and squeezed him close. 'Well Boaz, *you* happened next! After I was rescued along with your aunties and uncles, the spies welcomed us just like they promised. I met your father. And before long the Promised Land became my home, even though I was just an outsider.'

'You're not an outsider. You are a great hero!' Boaz said and snuggled into the warmth of his mother's body. 'Please tell me the story again.'

There are many Rahabs in the world: outsiders who are bullied by people around them, and feel useless and worthless. God noticed Rahab and kept her safe because he had a great plan for her life. You can read her story in Joshua 2 and Joshua 6, but she also gets an extra special mention in Matthew 1, Hebrews 11 and James 2.

JED'S STORY

The first time we met Jed he was on a play date. He had been on that play date for three whole weeks because his dad had not come back to pick him up. Sadly, this was the sort of play date Jed was used to. Sometimes the play dates would last days, sometimes weeks, and sometimes months. He had spent most of his life waiting for his dad to collect him from one place or another. Jed came to live with us while we looked for someone to adopt him and give him a place he could really call home. But nobody wanted to adopt Jed. Everyone thought that because of the colour of his skin he would end up in a gang or in prison.

But skin colour doesn't get to decide what you will be in life. Jed's auntie knows that. She adopted Jed in the end and tells me that at school he gets top grades in everything. She thinks that one day he will become the UK's first black prime minister.

Ehud's story is not that different from Jed's. He knew what it was like to be left behind too. God hadn't forgotten him either — he had great plans for his life.

EHUD

THE TALE OF THE BOY WHO WAS LEFT BEHIND

L eft. Right. Left. Right. Left. Right.

Have you ever seen soldiers marching perfectly in sync? It's a pretty awesome sight, in any country, in any period of history. The Benjaminite army 2,000 years ago was no exception. Whenever they paraded through town, everyone stopped to marvel.

Left. Right. Left. Right. Left. Right.

They were smart. They were slick. They were scary.

'But are they strong enough?' asked a voice in the crowd.

Everyone knew that not far away another army was poised ready to attack. That army was so strong and mighty, it had defeated all the other armies for miles around. It belonged to King Eglon the Evil, who was the greediest king you could ever imagine. However many soldiers he had in his army, he always wanted more. However many countries he invaded, he always wanted more. Even though he was the richest and most powerful person he knew, he always wanted more money and more power. Enough was never enough when it came to King Eglon the Evil.

'I'll help you defeat King Eglon the Evil,' piped up a small boy in the crowd, waving a stick and pretending to march like the soldiers of the Benjaminite army.

The crowd laughed and carried on their business and the small boy's dad ushered him home for his afternoon nap.

That small boy's name was Ehud. He loved watching the soldiers on parade. Every year on his birthday he would ask his dad if he was old enough yet to join the army. Every year his dad would shake his head, and Ehud would run into the garden to sulk and march by himself and play with his sticks. Well, if

the army wouldn't train him to be a soldier, then he would just have to train himself.

Ehud took his training very seriously.

He practised swinging his sticks until he could swat flies buzzing in the garden with his eyes shut.

He practised throwing his sticks until he could hit a target 30 metres away.

He practised juggling his sticks
until he could do five at a time
while hopping on one foot.

'Look, Dad!' Ehud would
shout, 'Look what I can do now!
I'm the best soldier ever!'

Ehud's dad tried to say
something encouraging from the
kitchen window. But he always
looked worried.

'Are you sure you want to
join the army?' he would ask.
'Don't you want to consider a
different career?'

Still there was no stopping Ehud. And eventually one birthday his dad... *nodded*. Yes! He was old enough to join the army. With a whoop and a cheer, Ehud ran to the barracks and signed himself up. He was ready to go anywhere, fight anyone and help get rid of greedy King Eglon the Evil.

Later that day, he ran home again. This time he wasn't whooping and cheering. This time he was sobbing and crying.

'Never mind, Ehud,' his dad said, wiping his son's nose with a rag. 'It's alright.'

'It's not alright at all,' Ehud cried. 'All my hard work practising was pointless. None of my dreams will come true. And everybody just laughs at me all the time.'

Ehud picked up one of his favourite sticks. He had spent hours whittling away at it with a knife so it looked just like a sword. He threw it as hard as he could. It was so sharp it whooshed right through the wall and out the other side, narrowly missing his pet dog that was sleeping in the flowerbed.

The sword landed in a ditch and disappeared beneath the water with a glug.

The reason Ehud's first day as a soldier had gone so badly was because of a Benjaminite army rule that he had known nothing about. All soldiers had to be right-handed. Ehud was left-handed.

'Apparently "right is right,"' Ehud moaned to his dad. 'Apparently "left is wrong. Left is weird. Left is banned."'

Now I know what you're probably thinking. This is ridiculous! It doesn't matter if you're right-handed or left-handed. People can do exactly the same jobs, and be just as brilliant, whichever hand they use. No one should feel worthless and left out just because of their hand preference.

You're right, but sadly, throughout history, people have been made to feel worthless and left out for all sorts of ridiculous reasons:

For being a girl. For being dark-skinned. For having freckles. For having ginger hair. For having one parent. For living on a particular side of town. For wearing bright clothes.

For having a certain accent. For having an unusual laugh.

None of these are good reasons to make anyone feel left out. In fact, the things that make us different can actually be the things that help make the world a better place.

But left-handed Ehud in an army with right-handed rules didn't know that yet.

'Right,' said his dad. 'Err, I mean, come on! Let's start practising with your right hand right away. Maybe you can get better.'

Ehud's second day as a soldier was not better at all. In fact it couldn't have been worse. He tried using his right hand, but he was so much slower and clumsier than everyone else in the class. He soon found himself being thrown out of the army in disgrace.

'It wasn't really my fault,' Ehud told his dad with a sob. 'If they'd let me swordfight with my strong hand I wouldn't have mis-swung. Or lost balance. Or chopped off the teacher's ear.'

'It's not the end of the world, son,' Ehud's dad said as Ehud sat at the empty breakfast table the next day thinking it *was* the end of the world.

'You should have heard the names people called me, Dad. All I wanted to do was fit in. I never thought I'd be so left out.'

'I understand,' Ehud's dad said kindly. 'People called me names when I was a boy too.'

Ehud didn't look up. He began carving an extra-long stick until it had razor sharp-blades.

'And your great-grandfather Joseph had a tough time when he was your age. His 11 brothers really didn't like him very much.'

'I know,' Ehud mumbled, sanding down the stick so the hilt fit snugly into his left hand.

'And your great-great-grandfather Jacob disappeared for 20 years because he was scared what people thought of him.'

'*I get it Dad*. I do,' Ehud said. 'I just thought it would be different for me!'

Ehud's stick now looked remarkably similar to the other soldiers' swords, except it was the wrong way round. Instead of strapping it to his left leg like the right-handed soldiers did, he tied it to his right leg.

Ehud's dad was very worried about what his son might use that sword for if he had nothing better to do. So he called in some favours and got Ehud a job as a delivery boy in the barracks. Perhaps it would keep him out of trouble.

Left. Right. Left. Right. Left. Right.

While the soldiers marched, Ehud was sent on errands. He had to run here, wait there, carry this, fetch that, stand up, sit down, get things out, put things away, get things out again. *It was exhausting.* But by the end of the day Ehud had discovered he actually quite liked being a delivery boy. He had discovered all sorts of information.

He knew when everyone's birthday was. He knew which soldiers had got into trouble. He had even overheard top-secret military intelligence being discussed.

'Did you know, Dad,' Ehud whispered one evening, 'the whole country is going to run out of food within weeks. They think greedy King Eglon

the Evil has stolen all the supplies.'

Sure enough, before long, the shops were empty and cupboards were bare. Nobody knew what to do. If it carried on like this everybody would starve to death.

'Guess what, Dad. The officers are considering offering a reward to anyone who can assassinate King Eglon the Evil. They say his death is the only way to save our people.'

Surprise, surprise: nobody put themselves forward to assassinate King Eglon the Evil.

'You'll never believe it, Dad!' Ehud burst out as he arrived home late one night. 'King Eglon the Evil has moved into that new palace in the town just up the road. He's throwing people out of their homes, turning all the children into his slaves and threatening to come here next. The army officers are having an emergency meeting with the town council right now to come up with a plan.'

The plan was weak, but it was all they could come up with under the circumstances. As the army wasn't anywhere near strong enough to fight King Eglon, they had no choice but to collect all their most valuable objects and present them as a gift. Perhaps if it was a good enough gift King Eglon would decide to be their friend.

Nobody had ever heard of King Eglon being friends with anyone. And everybody knew that real friendship couldn't be bought with a gift. But it was their only hope.

Now all that was left was to find someone who was willing to risk their life and deliver the gift to the King. The soldiers from the Benjaminite Army had a quick vote amongst themselves to decide whose life was the least important. There was a clear winner.

Ehud, the delivery boy, was perfect for the job.

'At least you haven't been left out this time,' Ehud's dad said to his son, who had hurtled through the door in a cold sweat and was shivering in a heap under the kitchen table.

He was still there the next morning when the army turned up at his door to escort Ehud and the gift to King Eglon the Evil. Well, most of the way to King Eglon the Evil.

Ehud's dad gave him a long, teary goodbye and then Ehud, dressed very smartly in an army uniform, set off on his miserable mission.

Left. Right. Left. Right. Left. Right …

… went the Benjaminite army.

Although, if you looked closely, you would have noticed one of the soldiers marching differently:

Right. Left. Right. Left. Right. Left.

HALT!!!!

The guards blocked the entrance to the palace King Eglon the Evil had stolen for himself. They checked every soldier's left leg. Any swords they found were confiscated. Then the soldiers waited and waited outside in the hot sun until finally King Eglon the Evil agreed to accept the gift.

Ehud entered the throne room and let out a gasp of astonishment. A huge banqueting table piled high with food took up most of the very large room. There were whole fish and steaming roast dinners and enormous cakes and towers of fruit and vegetables. There were jugs of drinks and dishes of sides and sweets and sauces. Servants ran in and out bringing more plates of all sorts of exotic food the likes of which Ehud had never seen before.

It was all for just one person.

At the end of the table sat greedy King Eglon the Evil. He was so busy stuffing his face with pork sausages he hardly noticed Ehud walking in to present his gift.

Ehud felt himself getting angrier and angrier as he got closer and closer to King Eglon the Evil. As fat dribbled down the King's extra-large chin he thought of all the people he knew whose stomachs had been empty for weeks. He remembered all the times he and his dad had had to share a crust of bread for dinner, while here the King sat, feasting on food he hadn't even prepared. Anything not to his taste, he threw on the floor! How could he sit there and eat like a pig, while people were starving? It wasn't right at all.

An idea began to form in Ehud's head. It was risky. It was illegal. It was unlikely to work. He would probably get killed in the process. But it was worth it. He was prepared to sacrifice his own life so that thousands of other lives could be saved.

'Excuse me, Your Majesty,' Ehud whispered as he laid the gift down at his feet. 'I've got a secret message for you.'

Now if there's one thing greedy, evil kings really love, it's finding ways to be even more greedy and evil. King Eglon the Evil looked down at Ehud and licked his lips. He wanted to hear this secret message. And he wanted to be the only one to hear the secret message. He gave the signal that he needed to use the bathroom, and the servants and visitors and guards and waitresses and chefs all politely left the room.

Except Ehud.

When everyone had gone, Ehud got up and locked the door behind them.

The King beckoned Ehud to come closer. And closer. And even closer. Soon Ehud was so close he could smell the king's bad breath. He could see the greasy stains on the king's napkin. He could even hear the king's bulging belly rumbling.

Leaning in as if to whisper his secret message, Ehud stretched his right hand around the king's broad shoulders.

With his left hand, Ehud pulled out the sword that was tied to his right leg and plunged it into King Eglon the Evil's belly. There it disappeared from the tip to the hilt with an almighty glug.

Saliva began to dribble down the dying King's chin. Blood started to seep through his tunic. And down below something brown and smelly oozed down his legs. King Eglon the Evil opened his huge greedy mouth for the last time and stopped breathing.

Ehud didn't waste a moment. He ran to the edge of the room and squeezed himself through one of the narrow

openings in the palace wall. He jumped to the ground, he sprinted into the woods and he ran all the way home, where he leapt into his bed and hid shaking beneath the covers.

'It's a miracle, son!' Ehud's dad said as he came in with a plateful of breakfast the next day. 'King Eglon the Evil is dead and our country is officially at peace. The farmers even managed to get food into town this morning without being robbed on the way.'

'Does anyone know how he died?' Ehud asked from under his blanket. His voice was unusually high and squeaky.

'It's a mystery, son!' Ehud's dad took a bite of toast. 'Some say he was assassinated by a highly skilled secret agent who moved like the shadows and vanished like the wind. Others say that he was killed by an invisible force with an invisible sword. Apparently there was blood everywhere but no weapon could be found.'

'I'm sure the guards must have their suspicions.'

93

'The guards have been fired. It seems there was such a terrible smell they thought he was busy on one of his frequent extra-long bathroom visits. They didn't go in for hours.'

Ehud's dad laughed, then he stood up and headed off to do the washing-up.

'Of course,' he called back from the doorway, 'everyone in this town knows exactly who saved the world from the rotten King Eglon the Evil.'

That day the celebrations began. All the stolen food was brought back from King Eglon the Evil's storehouses and the supplies didn't run out for decades.

As for Ehud, he was quickly discovered in his hiding place under the blankets and made an honorary soldier. Then he was promoted. First to captain. Then to commander. Then to high judge in charge of the whole country.

Ehud's dad told everyone that his son made a great high judge: nobody was ever left out, and most people did the right thing.

Even though everybody thought Ehud was useless, God picked him to help protect his people. So although Ehud felt left out with his left hand, he ended up being in exactly the right place at the right time.

You can read the original account of Ehud and Eglon in Judges 3.

KATY'S STORY

Katy was born with a condition that affects her legs. Even though she has had many operations, Katy has to go to school in a wheelchair and may need one for the rest of her life. Sometimes she wishes she could run around like everyone else. She finds it most frustrating when she can't join in with her friends.

Katy

But there are plenty of things Katy can do. She can ace her schoolwork, she can look after her brothers and sisters, she can keep everyone entertained at a party and she can certainly win an argument.

Katy is amazing. We think Katy would get on very well with the boy in the following story – they both know what it's like to be welcomed into a family who loves them just the way they are and helps them shine.

97

MEPHIBOSHETH

THE TALE OF THE CHILD WHO
HAD NOTHING TO LOSE

K nock knock!'
　　'Who's there?'
　　'Ziba'

If you're expecting a joke at this point, you'll be
disappointed. If it were not Ziba at the door, but someone
called 'Atch' or 'Boo' or 'Europe', you might have laughed.

Atch-who?

Boo-who?

Europe-who?

That might have been funny.

Unfortunately it was Ziba at the door. The Ziba who never
made anyone laugh. The Ziba who made babies cry even when
he didn't look at them. The Ziba who could give grown men
nightmares. The Ziba whose sinister smile would make your
hair stand up on end. The Ziba who would push you under a

bus if it helped him cross the road.

If Ziba ever knocks on your door, be sure not to let him in.

The boy cowering in fright in the cold, dark room had no intention of letting Ziba in either. But Ziba had a key. The boy heard it turning in the lock. He peeped through his shaking fingers as the heavy wooden door creaked open.

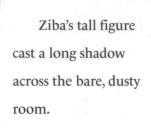

Ziba's tall figure cast a long shadow across the bare, dusty room.

The boy held his breath. Even the spiders scurried away to hide.

'Stand up, boy!' the unwelcome visitor demanded.

The boy's name was Mephibosheth. But nobody called him that. Nobody called him anything. Ziba was his only visitor and he couldn't be bothered with a long name like 'Mephibosheth'.

He couldn't be bothered to help Mephibosheth in any way whatsoever. He never gave him any clean clothes or soap to wash with. He didn't even give him anything to clip his nails with. Ziba only bothered with himself. So when he saw the boy, he saw an opportunity to make his own life better.

'I SAID STAND UP!'

Mephibosheth shuddered. He couldn't have stood up even if he'd wanted to, as Ziba knew full well.

'Hurry up, boy! I can't wait all day. I've got a reward to collect.'

Ziba reached into his long cloak, pulled out a crumpled poster and threw it on the floor. It read:

HUGE REWARD
Offered
For information
regarding the whereabouts
of any surviving members
of the former Royal
Family
of King Saul.

'This is what I've been waiting for since the day I met you!' Ziba grinned and rubbed his hands together. 'Finally my patience is going to pay off!'

Mephibosheth shuddered as he remembered that fateful day. It had begun as an ordinary morning not long after his fifth birthday. He had woken his dad up, as usual, by jumping on his bed and bouncing up and down. Then he had run into his grandfather's office, and tried to keep up with him as he did his morning exercises.

But their family breakfast together had been interrupted. A message had arrived warning that a battle was brewing. Because Mephibosheth's father was the Prince and his grandfather was the King, they had to go and help sort it out.

Mephibosheth had waited and waited for them to come home.

They never did.

Instead the enemy soldiers marched into the palace intending to wipe out the rest of the Royal Family.

Just in time, a kind and brave servant girl saw Mephibosheth and knew she couldn't leave him behind to be slaughtered. She picked him up and rushed out of the palace through the servant quarters. But in her panic she tripped.

As Mephibosheth tumbled down the hard stone steps the bones in his legs cracked and shattered. But even though he screamed out in pain, the girl was determined not to let the enemy soldiers find him and finish him off. At great risk to her own life, she managed to get him into the woods. There a tall man with strong arms offered to help her. He scooped the boy up and the kind and brave servant girl disappeared.

I think you've probably already guessed that that tall man was Ziba.

Instead of taking Mephibosheth to a doctor, he took him

to a place in the middle of nowhere called Lo-Debar, which means *Nothingland*. There he dumped the boy in a small dingy hut where nobody would ever find him. The boy's broken legs stayed broken. He never walked again.

There was nothing good about life in Nothingland. Nothing grew there. Nothing happened there. Ten long years went by and nothing gave Mephibosheth even the slightest hope that his life would get any better.

Every so often Ziba would turn up to check the boy was still alive and remind him that he had nothing to live for. Except, of course, to be exchanged for a reward that Ziba alone would enjoy.

'Finally our time has come!' Ziba said, laughing his most evil laugh. 'Apparently the new King of Israel can't wait to meet you. As soon as he makes sure you are dead, his throne will be safe for his own sons. And I'll get the reward I've been waiting for all these years.'

Mephibosheth wanted to ask Ziba for mercy, but he knew it was no use. He wanted to run away, but that was impossible too.

He felt himself being hauled up by Ziba and thrown over the back of his horse. They set off for the city. On the way Mephibosheth had to listen to Ziba's terrifying stories about the King.

'They say the King used to kill bears and lions with his bare hands when he was only eight years old.'

Mephibosheth bit his fingernails until he didn't have any more fingernails left to bite.

'Everyone knows the King once defeated a fearsome giant with only a handful of stones.'

Mephibosheth twisted and pulled his hair until he didn't have any more hair to twist and pull.

'The women in the marketplace keep count of the number of people the King has destroyed. They say it comes to tens of thousands.'

Mephibosheth shook in fear until he had no energy to shake in fear any more. If only his legs worked. Then he would jump down off the back of the horse. He would land on his feet. He would boot Ziba into oblivion. He would run far, far away from this terrifying, giant-slaying warrior King.

Mephibosheth was praying that his legs would somehow

carry him to safety when they
arrived at the King's palace.

Ziba pulled the boy off
the horse and dragged him backwards by his collar to the room
where the King was waiting.

'Your Majesty,' Ziba said, with a grand and rather smug
bow. 'In return for the promised reward, I offer you the only
surviving member of the former Royal Family of King Saul.
This deceitful boy was Prince Jonathan's son. He has been
hiding from you all these years. Now, thanks to me, you can
finally get rid of him.'

The King, who had been singing and playing a small harp
by his window, suddenly stopped and put down his instrument.
He rushed over to take a closer
look at the boy crumpled up on
the floor at Ziba's feet.

Mephibosheth didn't dare look up. That sword! It seemed dangerously close. And it looked dangerously sharp.

'Mephibosheth?' the King asked. 'Is it really you? How have you survived? Where have you been?'

Mephibosheth was too terrified to move. Was the King about to kill him with that dangerously sharp sword, with a giant-stunning stone or with his big, bare, bear-killing hands?

'I …' Mephibosheth stuttered. 'I am … I mean … I was … the son of Prince Jonathan. But I am no threat to you, Your Majesty. See? I can't even walk.'

Mephibosheth finally dared to look up briefly. And he saw something he wasn't expecting. The King's eyes had filled with tears.

'Your father was the best friend I ever had. Many years ago I promised him that I would take care of his family. Now I can fulfil that promise! Thank you, Mephibosheth. You've made me so happy.'

'Wait a minute!' Ziba interrupted. He scratched his head. He couldn't work out if the King was happy or sad, but he certainly didn't seem about to kill the boy. 'Haven't you seen his legs? Look at how crooked and broken they are. You don't want this burden in your life. He's just an embarrassment. In my opinion he's better off dead.'

Mephibosheth hung his head. 'Your Majesty, he's right. I'm worthless. I have nothing to offer you. I don't deserve your kindness.'

'Let me tell you about your family,' the King said, sitting
down on the cold floor next to Mephibosheth. 'When I was
about the same age as you, your father befriended me. Even
though it was dangerous for him. Even though he was a prince,
and I was a nobody. He believed that God had great plans for
me. He was a wonderful friend.'

Nobody had ever spoken to Mephibosheth about his father
like that before. Mephibosheth started to feel a little less scared.

'I will never forget the day your father found out that you
were on the way,' the King continued. 'He was so excited. And as
God knit you together in your mother's womb, he had already
fallen in love with you. I saw how he held you when you were
a baby. You couldn't walk then either, but your father knew
you were fearfully and wonderfully made. He would have been

so proud of you today. Please, stay here in the palace with me! Unless you've got somewhere else to go?'

Ziba couldn't believe his ears. This worthless child didn't deserve the King's attention. Finally he exploded.

'Is this a joke?

'How can you be serious?'

'WHAT ABOUT ME?'

'Ah yes, Ziba!' the King replied. 'I will reward you now. I hereby bestow upon you the very great honour of becoming Prince Mephibosheth's personal assistant. You are to make sure he gets whatever he needs, day or night.'

'But ... But ...'

Ziba and his buts were soon put to work. For the next 10 years, the new Prince lived in luxury in the King's palace. He ate at the King's table. He mixed with the King's guests. He had the same privileges as all the other princes in the land.

And for all those 10 years, Ziba ran around doing errands for Mephibosheth night and day with a big scowl on his face.

If you were expecting that to be the happy ending, you'd be wrong. You see, if Ziba could wait years and years for a reward, he could also wait years and years for his revenge.

One dreadful morning, the opportunity arose.

Mephibosheth had woken up to a commotion. There were voices yelling in panic outside his window.

'Emergency!'

'Somebody wants to kill the King!'

'We've got to get him to safety!'

'Where are we going?'

Mephibosheth called for Ziba to help him get up from his bed. But for the first time in 10 years Ziba didn't appear. When Mephibosheth finally heard Ziba's voice it was coming from the courtyard outside.

'Mephibosheth is refusing to get up, Your Majesty. He must be part of the plot to kill you. Leave that traitor for me – I'll deal with him.'

The day the King left was the day life went back to the way it had been all those years ago in Nothingland. Mephibosheth was trapped once again. He couldn't wash. He couldn't cut his hair. He couldn't even trim his nails. Ziba stormed in from time to time to tease him and torture him and torment him.

But this time things were different. Mephibosheth refused to let Ziba take away the little bit of hope that was left inside him.

He remembered how God hadn't forgotten him when he was a boy and he prayed that God wouldn't forget him this time. He remembered those stories Ziba had once told him: how the King had killed bears with his bare hands; how he had defeated tens of thousands of soldiers; how he had even slain a giant. Those stories had scared him last time, but now they gave him courage. God had helped the King before. God would help him again.

More days, more weeks and more months passed with no news.

Then one day…

'Knock knock!'

'Who's there?'

'The King.'

Mephibosheth was tired of Ziba playing this cruel joke. But he had to reply or Ziba would punish him.

'The King who?'

'The King who?!' repeated a voice that didn't sound like Ziba's. *'The King who?!!'* The King Who Just Reclaimed His Kingdom. The King Who Wants to Know Why You Didn't Come With Me? The King Who Can't Believe That You Betrayed Me. The King Who Missed You. The King Who Wants to Put Everything Right Again.'

The door burst open. It *was* the King! He looked at Mephibosheth with his messy clothes and dirty face and long nails – and he embraced him just as warmly as he had done all those years ago. It was time to celebrate all over again.

And what do you think happened to Ziba?

Well, fortunately for him, Mephibosheth and the King were **so happy** just to be together again, they couldn't be bothered to take revenge on him. In fact Mephibosheth and the King were **so happy**, they even agreed to give Ziba the reward he was so desperate to get his hands on.

Perhaps that made Ziba happy for a while. But I expect he quickly discovered that no amount of riches would make him ever as happy as the King and Mephibosheth were when they were together.

You can read this story in 2 Samuel 4, 9 and 19. Perhaps you could read Luke 14 afterwards where Jesus describes the surprising people who get invited to eat at the royal table of the King of Kings.

EMMA'S STORY

Emma used to be top of her class. She had the neatest handwriting, the best spelling and the loudest laugh. Everyone wanted to play with Emma. When she wasn't out with one of her many friends, she was at gymnastics training. She could jump and bounce and somersault like you wouldn't believe. Every weekend she would show us the shiny medals she had won for her shows and competitions.

Emma

When Emma was ten, her life changed. First she got an injury and lost a few weeks of gymnastics practice. Then she lost someone she loved very much. Soon after that she lost her confidence too. She became anxious about school, then too scared to leave the house.

One day, we hope that Emma will become bubbly and bouncy again. In the meantime perhaps she can relate to the girl in this story, who also found the world a difficult place to live in.

THE SAMARITAN
THE TALE OF THE GIRL WHO DIDN'T FEEL WELL

The girl peeped through the curtains of her darkened house at the end of the street. She saw no one, and nobody saw her. Breathing a sigh of relief, she pulled a cloak over her head. Hopefully she could get to the well and back without being seen.

It had been 634 days since she had spoken to anyone.

It had been 634 days since anyone had spoken to her.

Unfortunately that hadn't stopped people speaking *about* her. Some mornings the girl could hear the mums warning their children not to go anywhere near her. Some afternoons she could hear the children daring each other to touch her gate, before screaming and running away. And in the evenings she

heard the men laughing together in the street. She could just feel that she was the butt of their jokes.

The girl would lock her door, blow out her candle and shudder under her blanket, knowing the next day would be just the same, or even worse.

If anyone has called you names, you might know a little bit what it felt like to be this girl. Maybe you've walked into a room to an awkward hush and guessed that people have been talking about you. Perhaps you've seen children pointing at you from across the playground. Or perhaps your dreams are filled with people laughing at you or ignoring you, pitying you or picking on you. It can make you feel angry. It can make you feel scared. You know this is not the way the world is supposed to be. The world is supposed to feel safe. It's supposed to make you want to live your life to the full.

The girl picked up her bucket, walked to her front door and counted down from 10.

'Ten. Nine …'

She really didn't want to leave the house, but she had to get the water. Nobody saw her last time. Or the time before. It was probably safe to go.

'Eight. Seven …'

At least the dogs had stopped barking. That was a good sign. She prayed silently that nobody would see her.

'Six. Five …'

She put her hand on the

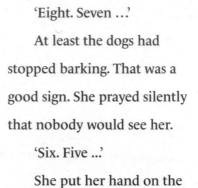

doorknob and waited for her heart rate to slow down again. Why was it so hard to do this every day?

'Four. Three …'

She opened the door just

a crack and checked again that nobody was there. In the distance she could see the holy mountain where she used to go, laughing and running and climbing. How she wished she

could go again, but maybe she never would. She could hardly manage to get to the end of her street.

'Two. One ...'

She stepped out onto her doorstep, closed the door quietly behind her and hurried off towards the well as fast as her legs would carry her.

The girl stared at the ground as she ran so moving shadows wouldn't scare her. It was hot and her bucket was heavy even though it was empty. She longed to drink some of the cool water she would find at the well. But she would wait until she was safely back in her house.

When she was younger, going to the well was her favourite thing. Her mum used to give her a small bucket to carry and they would joke and sing as they skipped down the street. When they arrived, she always played with her friends, hoping the grown-ups would chat a very long time. She was rarely disappointed. The women always had lots of local gossip to share, problems to solve, and news to discuss.

Then as they walked slowly home with their heavy buckets, her mum would tell her stories. There was one about how God helped a man called Noah sail to the holy mountain on a boat

in a flood. There was another about a woman called Sarah whose son nearly died on the holy mountain. There was one about a warrior called Joshua. The holy mountain, so she was told, was where he had won loads of battles.

But the best one was a story about the Messiah.

'Miss who?' the girl joked.

'Messiah means "Sent from God"', her mum proudly explained. 'You know, one day God will send a Messiah to welcome us into his family, show us the truth and fix the world.'

'But the world isn't broken,' the girl always replied. To her, life with her mum and friends and small bucket of water seemed perfect. 'So the Messiah can't come yet.'

In the years that followed, the girl was to discover just how terribly broken the world actually was. When her mum died, she was sent away, and there followed a series of very unfortunate events, each worse than the one before.

The girl running towards the well tried not to think about those unfortunate events. She had to concentrate. She carefully tiptoed past a pack of sleeping dogs.

She skirted around the dangerous potholes.

She ducked under the wind chimes outside the café.

And she held her nose trying not to sneeze as she raced by the wild meadow.

When she finally arrived at the well, she wasted no time in lowering her bucket down on a rope. It plopped into the water and sank beneath the surface. If she could just pull it up again quickly, she could run back home to safety.

As the girl looked at her reflection in the bottom of the well she jumped and almost dropped the rope: another face was staring back at her.

'Hello, young lady,' the face said.

The girl's heart raced faster than usual. She didn't dare look up. Beside her at the well was her worst nightmare.

It was a person. An actual person.

Not only that. It was a man.

Not only that. It was a man from out of town.

Not only that. It was a man from out of town who was speaking. *To her!*

Not only that. She was alone.

'You *can* talk to strangers,' her mum had always said, 'but be careful. Stick with your friends, and if the stranger makes you uncomfortable, walk away.'

The girl pulled her cloak down and looked around. For

the first time in 634 days, she wished she had a friend to stick with. A friend to chat to. A friend to walk away with. She began hauling her bucket up but her hands were shaking so much, most of the water spilled out.

'Would you mind giving me a drink, young lady?' The stranger had a kind voice, but the girl knew that didn't mean

he wasn't trouble – specially with that accent. 'Why would you ask *me* for a drink, sir?' she said. 'I know your accent and your people don't talk with my people.'

'Why *wouldn't* I ask you for a drink?' asked the stranger. 'More importantly, why wouldn't you ask *me* for a drink?'

The girl didn't know what to say. How could she tell him she never asked anyone for anything? If it wasn't for this frightening well visit every day, she would stay at home and never speak to anyone ever again. If only she could wish herself back to the refuge that was her bedroom. Along with a never-ending supply of fresh water. Or a pill that meant she would never be thirsty again. Of course, that was about as likely as discovering the magical fountain of eternal life. Nothing like that ever happened in real life.

'Well?' said the man.

'Well...' replied the girl, peering down to the bottom of the

one right in front of her. 'I wouldn't ask you for water, sir. Because, for a start, you don't have a bucket. Or a rope.'

An odd picture filled her head. It involved

the man diving headfirst
into the well, scooping up
water with his bare hands,
then climbing out using
only his feet and elbows.
There'd hardly be a drop left
by the time he got back up.

'But I do have water,' the
man said. 'Trust me. I have a
never-ending supply of fresh
water. With my water you
would never be thirsty again.
It would be your own fountain
of eternal life.'

It had been a long time since the girl had spoken to someone else. Precisely 634 days. But as far as she could remember, conversations didn't usually involve mind-reading. Or people claiming they needed a drink while simultaneously boasting about a personal, eternal and magical water supply.

Despite the growing strangeness of the stranger, the girl found herself beginning to feel safer than she had felt in a long time. Her heart was beating fast, but it felt different to normal. Warmer. The man was speaking without any hint of cruelty. He wasn't putting her down or teasing her or bullying her or judging her.

There was something else too. It was almost as though she knew him already. But, of course, that was impossible. She had to focus on what was real, on the facts.

'Did you know,' she found herself saying rather nervously, 'that this well was built by a man called Jacob? He lived hundreds of years ago and once met God quite unexpectedly by

a river. My family has been coming
to this well for generations.'

'I know,' the man replied. Then he
asked: 'Can I meet your family?'

The girl jumped. It would have been a polite question to anyone else, but it cut like a knife into her heart. The series of unfortunate events that had ripped her family apart over the years was the last thing she wanted to talk about. She was sure it would only lead to trouble. She pulled the cloak up over her face again, and picked up the heavy bucket only half full of water.

'Sir, please give me your super-water so I don't need to come back here ever again,' she said quietly. It was worth a shot.

'It's all right,' the man said softly. 'I know about your family.'

The girl looked sideways at the man. She had kept so much secret over the years. The only person she had trusted with her family problems was God. Had God passed on her information to this stranger? Was he a prophet? She found herself remembering her mum and the stories she used to tell. The girl's eyes wandered to the holy mountain in the distance – was this an extraordinary man like the people from the holy mountain stories?

'The mountain is irrelevant,' the man said.

There it was again. He was reading her mind! The girl was starting to realise this was no ordinary stranger.

'What sort of God wants people running up and down mountains anyway?' he continued. 'What's the point in that? God is looking for people to welcome into his family, who will show the truth and help him fix the world.'

That was exactly what her mother used to say!

'Are you talking about the Messiah?' she asked. 'The one who is supposed to be sent from God?'

'I *am* talking about the Messiah! And you, young lady, are talking *to* the Messiah.'

The girl gasped.

What were the chances that after 634 days of talking to nobody, she would find herself talking to the Messiah, sent from God! Could it be true? She could almost believe it. Except she'd always imagined the Messiah would have had many followers who'd given up everything to be with him.

Just at that moment, a whole crowd of people turned up. They reminded her a lot of the men who had fought with her father. But none of them mentioned the holy-mountain feud. They didn't even criticise the man for talking with a girl like her. They didn't laugh at her, put her down, turn their noses up at her or avoid eye contact with her. Instead, they greeted her kindly.

It was as if the world was beginning to get fixed.

'Wait there. I'll be right back,' the girl said, leaving her cloak and her bucket next to the well. 'Oh, and help yourself to water,' she called over her shoulder. As she ran up the street she hardly felt the ground beneath her feet.

She raced back past the wild meadow, forgetting to hold her nose.

She skipped through the twinkling wind chimes outside the café.

She leapt over the dangerous potholes and sprinted right through the middle of the surprised pack of dogs.

When the girl got to her house she didn't stop. Instead she began knocking frantically on her neighbours' doors. One by one they came out wondering what on earth was going on. Soon the whole town was in the street to see what had happened to the strange girl who was out and about for the first time in years.

'Did you say you're not feeling well?' someone asked her.

'I said there's a man at the well,' she repeated. For once, she didn't really mind that they were all staring at her.

'This man knows everything about me. Everything! I think he's the Messiah. You all have to come and meet him!' If you had been there in Samaria that day, you would have followed the girl back to the well too. Clearly, something ***extra-ordinary*** was going on.

'Thank you, Jesus!' she said at the end of the day after everyone had been and gone. 'I believe this town is never going to be the same again.'

'Thank *you*,' Jesus said. 'People came to see me because of you. You're not so invisible after all. And one day the whole world will know who you are.'

'Really?' The girl still felt like the world was a scary place, but maybe not quite as scary as it had felt earlier in the day. 'I'm not sure I am ready for the whole world to know who I am. Can you at least keep my name secret?'

'I understand,' Jesus said. 'Nobody else needs to know your name. But I will never forget it. I will secretly write it on the palm of my hand until the day we meet again.'

The difficult things that have happened to us in the past don't need to stop us looking forward to the future. Read this story for yourself in John 4 and see how Jesus can change lives.

LIAM'S STORY

When Liam was a baby he cried when he was put down. When he was a toddler he was scared of his own reflection. The first time he went to a swimming pool he thought he was going to drown.

When Liam started primary school he was convinced elephants were going to crash through the roof because of a story his teacher had read to him.

When he started secondary school he thought something terrible would happen if he didn't cross his letter **t** in exactly the right place.

If you met Liam today in his art studio, you wouldn't even guess that he had so many worries. He has learned some great strategies that help him. Perhaps he could learn some more from the girl in this story, and her amazing guest.

MARTHA

THE TALE OF THE SISTER WHO WORRIED TOO MUCH

Did you know that worrying can be good for you? Worrying is what stops you from eating strange things you find lying in the road. Or kicking strangers in the street. Or jumping into deep and dangerous lakes. Worrying is what makes you run away from wild animals, and avoid going too close to the edge of dangerous cliffs. Worrying is a good sign that you are healthy and safe and your body wants you to stay healthy and safe.

But there are some people who worry too much. If worrying were an Olympic sport those people would come home with a gold medal. If there were exams in worrying, they would get top marks. If they were given a penny for every worry they had, they'd be millionaires.

Fortunately today there are experts around who can help children and adults understand and manage their anxieties and realise that most things are never as bad as they imagine.

Martha was in grave danger of becoming someone who worried much too much.

It started off with worries about little things like getting people's names wrong, wearing her clothes back to front or leaving her room untidy.

Then it turned into worries about silly things like imaginary mice sleeping under her bed, eyelashes falling into her food, and forks being muddled with the knives in the cutlery drawer.

She almost didn't have time to worry about big things like putting food on the table, paying her taxes and keeping her brother and sister safe.

Things got really bad when she started to worry that she was too worried, which made her even more worried. And if she ever ran out of things to worry about, she started to worry about why she had run out of things to worry about.

Martha's younger sister Mary and even her younger
brother Lazarus used to get very frustrated with Martha
for worrying so much.

'But what if a spider crawls into my mouth
in the night and I choke and the house catches
fire and I can't warn anybody and the whole
village burns down?' Martha would ask.

Mary would roll her eyes. 'Stop worrying so
much, Martha.'

'What if I forget to take my coat out on a
breezy day and I start sneezing and the whole
world catches my cold and the planet collapses
under the weight of all those used handkerchiefs?'

Lazarus would hold his hands up in the air in
dismay. 'Martha, stop worrying about everything.'

One day Martha was in the middle of worrying
about how quiet it was when there was a commotion
outside her window. That made her start worrying about
how noisy it was. Lazarus and Mary weren't worried. They were
really excited.

'It's the visitor everyone has been talking about. Apparently he tells stories and even heals people. Can we invite him for dinner?' Mary asked.

'Certainly not!' Martha glared at her sister in horror. 'What if we waste his important time? What if he thinks our house is a mess? What if he brings the whole crowd with him and we run out of food? What if he doesn't bring anyone and we end up alone with a stranger in the house? It's a terrible idea. Probably the most terrible idea you've ever had.'

But Mary and Lazarus weren't listening. They had just heard the man tell a story about helping strangers and were already on their way to offer him a meal and a place to sleep.

The visitor, whose name was Jesus, was very grateful for the delicious roast dinner that Martha, at rather short notice, had prepared.

'Come again!' Lazarus called out as he left the next day. And he did. Every time Jesus was in town he stayed with the three of them and soon they were all great friends.

One evening Martha was preparing dinner as usual and worrying as usual when Jesus came into the kitchen.

'I'm worried about Mary,' Martha blurted out. 'Why isn't she helping me? She knew we had bread to knead, and vegetables to chop and pans to wash and fruit to peel. Is she getting forgetful? Is she getting lazy? Doesn't she care about me any more? What if the food isn't ready on time, and all our visitors starve to death? What if you think we are terrible hosts and never come back? What if the whole village says it's our fault you've stopped coming to heal people? What if they throw us out of town?'

'Martha, Martha,' Jesus said as he began to scrub the dirty dishes. 'You worry much too much about too many things.'

That night Martha was sweeping the porch and still feeling cross. She didn't understand Jesus at all. One minute he was telling people to go around helping strangers, and the next he *wasn't* telling Mary to go and help her struggling sister.

It didn't make sense!

As Martha lay in bed feeling as confused and worried as she was cross, Jesus' words echoed around her head: 'Martha, Martha, you worry much too much about too many things.'

Why hadn't Jesus told her just to stop worrying like everyone else did?

If only Martha had asked him what he meant. If only she had taken time to listen more carefully. But she'd been rushing around the kitchen, trying to remember where she'd put the eggs and feeling cross with Mary.

Tomorrow would be different. She would ask Jesus everything she'd always wanted to ask him. Then she would sit and listen to all his answers, just like Mary had done.

But the next morning Jesus was gone.

Martha worried he would never come back.

149

Days and weeks went by. Mary and Lazarus missed him too. They couldn't stop talking about him. The things he had said. The people he had helped.

Finally Martha heard a rumour in the marketplace that Jesus was heading back into town. She ran home. She got all the food ready. She got all the bedding ready. She cleaned the house from top to bottom. The last room to do was Lazarus'.

But Lazarus didn't look very well. Martha called the doctor but by the time he arrived, Lazarus was even sicker.

'Don't worry,' Mary said, as Martha sat wiping Lazarus' head with cool cloths.

'Jesus is only a couple of miles away. He sent a message saying he's on his way and that Lazarus would be fine.'

Martha waited and waited and got more and more worried. By the end of the day Jesus still hadn't arrived. Then during the night – Lazarus died.

It was as though the world had stopped.

The two sisters cried until there were no more tears to cry.

Martha felt empty and cold even though the sun was shining. Her neighbours tried to comfort her but their words hurt. Everything hurt. It was as if she'd been punched in the stomach and kicked in the back at the same time.

'Why Lazarus?' Martha wailed. 'Why now? Where was Jesus when we needed him? Why would he leave one of his friends to die when he is always making time for strangers? I don't think I can ever forgive him.'

Before the end of the day
Lazarus' body was wrapped
in cloth and placed in the cave the town used as a grave. All
the neighbours came out to show their respects and the priest

called for the big stone
to be rolled back in
front of the entrance.

Martha felt worried
and sad and angry and
lonely. She didn't know what to do with herself.

A few long and difficult days later Martha heard a
commotion outside in the street. Rage burned in her chest as
she marched out of the house looking for Jesus.

'Where were you?' Martha shouted, barging through the
crowd. 'You said you were coming. You said Lazarus would be
fine. How could it take you five whole days to walk just two
miles? If you'd been here earlier, he wouldn't have died.'

Jesus hushed the crowd and gave Martha his full attention.

'Martha, Martha!' Jesus said. 'Your brother will rise again.'

'I believe that,' Martha replied with a sigh. 'I've heard you say many times that one day there will be a resurrection when everyone who has died will start a new life. And God will reunite us all in heaven. But what if I can't wait until then for that resurrection and life? If only that resurrection and life could turn up right here, right now! Wouldn't that be better?'

Jesus looked at Martha. His kind eyes met her confused eyes as he said

'I am the resurrection and the life.'

Martha shrugged and walked away. She really didn't understand Jesus. Was he claiming to be God now? At a time like this?

Later that afternoon, Mary and Martha went to visit Lazarus' grave. Martha was secretly pleased that Jesus was there. The least he could do was pay his respects, after all he had put them through.

'Look, Martha,' Mary whispered as they knelt together in

the garden. 'Jesus is crying.'

Sure enough tears were running down Jesus' cheeks. In that moment Martha stopped being cross with him. He had lost a friend, just as they had lost a brother.

'Look, Martha,' Mary whispered again. 'Jesus is asking to see Lazarus' body.'

Martha had been to enough funerals to know that some people liked to be able to see the body of their friends who had died. It was their way of saying goodbye. But nobody ever went after the first day because the body would be too rotten.

It was **four days** since Lazarus' body had been buried. It would look and smell terrible. This was going to be a very unpleasant experience.

'Why isn't he going inside the cave?' Martha whispered to Mary, holding her nose.

'Perhaps the smell is too bad,' Mary guessed. 'Maybe he's too upset. Maybe he feels guilty. Maybe he just can't face it.'

They didn't have to wait long to find out.

'Look, Mary!' Martha said, jumping up. 'Who's that with Jesus? It can't be? Can it?'

'Lazarus?'

'LAZARUS!'

Mary and Martha ran and hugged Lazarus and each other for a very long time. Martha felt as though the sun had come out even though it was late in the evening. It was as if a weight had been lifted off her shoulders and happiness was exploding out of her.

Jesus wasn't just a teacher and
healer. He *was* the resurrection and
life. *He was God!*

And Lazarus wasn't dead after
all. He was very much alive.

That night there was a huge celebration party. Lazarus was the guest of honour in his own house, but it was Jesus everyone wanted to talk to.

Martha was, for a change, a terrible hostess. She didn't serve any drinks or prepare any food, although somehow there was plenty to eat and drink. Instead she sat at Jesus' feet and listened. Every so often she squeezed Lazarus' hand to make sure he was still alive.

Later when everyone had gone home or gone to bed, Martha started to worry about breakfast. What if there wasn't enough milk, and Lazarus got a piece of dry toast stuck in his throat and couldn't breathe and they had to bury him all over again and Jesus' miracle became a big joke?

'I wish Jesus would heal you from worrying all the time, Martha,' Mary said, half asleep.

Martha considered this for a while. If Jesus could raise someone from the dead, he could certainly heal her from her anxiety. Then again, Martha knew Jesus accepted her just the way she was. Perhaps over time her worries would go away. That wasn't something she was going to worry about though. She had something much more important to do.

Even though Martha had not sat listening to Jesus like Mary had, she was determined not to forget the amazing things he had said to her. She wrote it all down carefully and pinned it up in her kitchen where she could keep it safe and read it often. Maybe one day someone would want to write a book about Jesus and the amazing things he said and did.

The words Jesus said to Martha were kept safe for thousands of years and still help people who are worried or grieving. You can read them for yourself in the Bible in Luke 10 and John 11.

MOLLY'S STORY

Molly is a beautiful girl whose favourite game is dressing up. When she is a sheriff, everyone does what they are told. When she is queen, everyone shows her respect. When she is a pop star, everyone listens and wants to take selfies with her. Molly was born with a rare condition that means her bones don't grow the same way as most people's.

Although she can do everything other children her age can do, she is really, really short.

Sometimes people stare at her or ask why she is so little. But Molly always smiles at them. She may be small on the outside but inside she is big-hearted.

I would love Molly to meet Zac from our next story. I think he — and the friend who eventually finds him — would make a big impression on her.

ZACCHAEUS

THE TALE OF THE CONMAN WHO WAS CAUGHT SHORT

Mr and Mrs Potter, of number 7 Wall Street, Jericho, liked to think their life was perfect. They had a large house filled with beautiful things, a shed in the garden where they had a small bowl-making business, and a big vegetable patch where Mr and Mrs Potter liked to potter in the evenings. The front of the house faced the large and rather wonderful Italian Winter Palace and there were always important people walking up and down their most desirable street.

The only thing missing from their perfect life was a perfect child. So imagine their joy when one spring morning just before tea Mrs Potter gave birth to a beautiful, bouncy baby boy. They named him Zacchaeus.

Zacchaeus was a name with a meaning: 'pure and innocent'. They called him Zac for short. What more could they want in life now they had a son who could do no wrong? So Mr and Mrs Potter settled back to watch Zac grow up, which he did to some extent. And when they eventually grew old and died, they did so still thinking their life – and son – were perfectly perfect.

Being an only child, Zac inherited everything. He became the sole owner of number 7 Wall Street and everything in it. You might think he would be happy with a life consisting mainly of sitting in the garden, munching on the produce of the well-prepared vegetable plot and enjoying the beautiful things around him. But Zac wasn't happy. Even though he had everything he needed, he did not have everything he wanted.

You see, when Zac was growing up, his bedroom didn't face the garden with the shed and the vegetables like that of his parents. When Zac opened the curtains in the morning, he had a view of the Italian Winter Palace. He could see gold vases in the windows, large wardrobes filled with beautiful clothes and tables always piled high with sumptuous banquets. Compared to all that his house felt very small and ordinary. The thought of getting his hands dirty on his parents' potter's wheel in the garden shed filled him with horror.

But Zac needed to earn money, so he got out a pen and paper and started to think of all the other jobs he could do instead. He wanted a job that paid not just well, but very well.

These were the jobs at the top of his list:

an internationally famous male supermodel

Apart from the fact that Zac had no experience in any of these careers, there was another problem. Zac was below average height. Well below average height.

And people of well below average height got rather overlooked when it came to applying for jobs like royal bodyguards, Olympic runners, army generals and male supermodels. Ironically enough, every time he applied **he didn't even make the shortlist.**

Now the world would be a particularly boring place if we were all identical. It's great that we're all different and come in all sorts of shapes and sizes. Some people love the shape and size they happen to be. Others don't. Sometimes they don't like their shape and size because of other people and the cruel

things they say about them. Sometimes
they struggle to like their shape and size,
even though others tell them they are
beautiful.

Zac didn't like being short.

He could never reach the cupboards
where the biscuit tin was kept.

He was never chosen for any of the
local sports teams.

He couldn't go on any of the rides at

the town funfair.

He couldn't
buy anything
from the top shelves in the
local store.

He couldn't even look down
his nose at people he didn't like.

When he realised he couldn't
do any of his dream jobs either, he
became more and more miserable.
And increasingly poor.

169

Zac had no choice. He went down to the garden shed and got out a large lump of clay. He threw it on the wheel, and covered it with water, just like he'd seen his parents do. As he squeezed his fingers knuckle deep into the red sludge, he had a thought. What if he could make beautiful vases instead of boring bowls? He imagined people coming from far and wide and paying millions for them. Just think. He could become rich and famous from the comfort of his own home!

But just as he'd started to think that being a potter might not be so bad, he realised he could never, ever be a potter. You know why, don't you? That's right. His legs didn't reach to the pedal that turned the wheel.

'Well that was another short-lived dream,'

Zac wiped his hands on his shirt and stomped back to the house. He was just in time to hear a knock at the front door.

'Taxes, please!' The visitor rattled a tin of coins in Zac's face.

Zac scowled. He hated parting with money. Especially money he didn't have. Or couldn't reach.

'Now then, Mr Potter, on the plus side you haven't sold any bowls recently, so you owe nothing in income tax. But I'm sorry to say that a war has just started on the southern border, and the army needs more funds. There's also road tax, the palace courtyard fund, the temple tax and crop taxes to pay. And as you've inherited this house recently I'm afraid there's rather a hefty sum owed. How about I round that up to…?'

Zac slammed the door. How was he supposed to get rich and famous if people kept taking his money away?

'I bet he keeps half of it for himself anyway,' Zac grumbled, glaring through the window at the taxman who was busy scribbling away on his notepad.

Suddenly Zac had an idea.

It wasn't just any old idea. It was the most brilliant idea he had ever had. It would solve all his problems in one fell swoop.

Zac opened the door, invited the taxman in and offered him a drink. And a deal.

That afternoon, Zac accompanied the man on his rounds. Soon every household in the street had not only discovered two visitors at their door but an extra charge on their bill.

'It's the new personal security tax,' Zac explained in one doorway after another. 'Just put the extra money in my tin and I'll make sure the rotten Roman soldiers don't come and get you in the middle of the night.'

By the end of the afternoon, Zac had a tin full of coins. It was still pretty full after he'd paid all his taxes, *and* given his new friend a generous bonus.

'You know, Zac,' his friend said, 'good tax collectors are currently in short supply.'

Zac went to bed that night feeling rather pleased with himself.

Over the next few years Zac the tax collector got even better at tricking his friends and neighbours. While they became poorer and poorer, he grew richer and richer. Of course, he also

grew more and more unpopular, but he didn't mind too much about that. Each night he would drool over his shiny new things and his growing piles of coins, and congratulate himself for being so greedy and stingy and selfish.

'I may be short, but at least I'm not short of cash,' he joked to himself.

Mr Zacchaeus Potter, of number 7 Wall Street, Jericho had finally got to the point where life seemed almost perfect. His garden was overgrown with weeds and the vegetable patch was bare but he didn't care. He was far too busy enjoying life as the Chief Extortion Officer of the firm 'Zac's Tax'. He not only had a brand he could be proud of and a reputation as the town's worst trickster, but a rather large stash of treasure to boot.

Almost five years to the day after his first afternoon working as a taxman's helper, Zac came out of a board meeting to some rather unpleasant news. There was a rumour of a new conman around. This new conman had been attracting huge crowds everywhere he went. Apparently he had people eating out of his hand. He had been seen preying on the poor. This new hustler even claimed he could heal the sick and give people a better life. Who wouldn't pay for that?

'How dare he!' Zac fumed. 'If people start putting their money in this guy's tin, they'll have nothing left for me.'

Zac marched straight
into town to see for
himself who it was that was
swindling on his patch.

It didn't take long for Zac to find a huge
crowd. He could hear someone speaking at the

front, but he
couldn't see anything. However much he jumped up and
down he couldn't even get a glimpse of this newcomer. However
much he pushed and jostled, he couldn't get any closer. If

only he was more
important, he could
have parted the crowd with
a command. If only he was more popular, the
townsfolk might have felt sorry for him stuck at the back with
no view. If only he was taller, he could have seen something
other than people's backs and bottoms.

Zac sighed, and leaned against a big,
leafy tree. He had to get higher up, but how?

If you had been there and suggested that he climb that tree, Zac would have argued with you. Climbing trees was dangerous. Climbing trees was difficult – especially when you didn't have long arms and legs. Climbing trees was daft – definitely not his style …

Although he did want to see who it was that had got the crowd's attention.

And that first branch was surprisingly low.

And nobody was watching.

Zac swung himself up.

But he still couldn't see over the heads of the crowd. So he climbed up onto the next branch.

By the time he'd reached the third branch Zac could see perfectly.

176

But he could also be seen.

So Zac clambered up to a fourth branch and hid out of sight high up in the leaves.

Zac could see everything from up there. He could see the conman talking. He could see the crowd – made up of everyone he had ever swindled. *And* he could see why they all loved and trusted this man. The promises he made! The stories he told! The sense he talked!

The one thing Zac couldn't see was any money changing hands. Not a single penny. No tin in sight. Where was the scam? Where was the hoax? Where was the swindle?

It was a hot afternoon. As the sun beat down, the speaker decided to find himself some shade under the biggest, leafiest tree in the street. Soon he was standing right below where Zac was hiding. From there he talked to the crowd about a world where people weren't greedy or selfish or stingy.

Zac felt the man was speaking directly to him. He was, after all, the greediest, stingiest, most selfish person he knew. Sure, he was rich, but he was also miserable. He had all the gold vases and beautiful clothes and sumptuous banquets he could ever wish for. But something big was still missing from his life.

Just as he was beginning to imagine what it would be like if people stopped looking down on him and began looking up to him, the whole crowd lifted their heads.

They looked up at Zac hiding in the tree.

The conman was pointing right at him.

'Zacchaeus!' he called up.

'Who, me?' Zac replied.

Zac had no idea how the conman knew his name. Or how he knew he was hiding in the tree. Or whether he was about to be pounced on by the crowd. Or why he had a sudden feeling that he wanted to get to know this man who saw life so differently to him.

'Come down, Zacchaeus! My name is Jesus and I've heard all about you.'

As Jesus looked up at Zac, and Zac looked down at Jesus, Zac realised that everything was the wrong way around. He deserved to be looked down on. He had made poor choices in life. He had got his priorities all wrong. He had fallen short.

'Can I come to your house tonight? I'd like to have dinner with you,' Jesus asked.

We don't know what
was on the menu that night.
We don't know who else was
invited. But we do know that
Zac's mealtime encounter with
Jesus was life-changing.

'All staff are to report to me
at once,' Zac announced to his
team the next morning. 'Today
we're going to go through the
accounts. Everyone we ever stole from will get a windfall of four
times the amount we took. It's payback time.'

When all the money was gone, Zac put up a big sign saying,
Zac's Tax: Closed for Business, wrote himself a
letter of resignation and went home walking taller than he had
ever done before.

Some time later you might have found Zac hanging out at the local church. You might even have noticed that he was helping to lead it. And you might have heard people saying how wonderful they found it when Zac preached. He knew all sorts of things about Jesus. He never asked for a penny. He put his own lessons into practice.

And he always kept his sermons short.

Meeting Jesus, spending time with him and learning to be generous because of his example is something people still discover they can do today. Read the original story in Luke 19.

AHMAD'S STORY

Ahmad arrived in our family one afternoon with a huge appetite, a wonderful smile and a great big scar on his body. It turned out he'd had an operation in a different country that had sadly caused more harm than good. The only thing the doctors could do for him was to do the operation all over again.

If you've ever had an operation you'll know that you can't eat anything for a whole day. Ahmad didn't enjoy that one bit. As

Ahmad

soon as the operation was over, we bought him the biggest cream cake he had ever seen. That cake didn't last long – but the scar is there forever.

Ahmad lives with his dad now. His dad says that the double scar may remind him of a difficult time in his life, but it also means that someone loved him enough to help him. This story is dedicated to Ahmad and children who have scars, visible and invisible, and need to know that someone loves them.

JESUS

THE TALE OF THE HEALER WHO WAS SCARRED FOR LIFE

Did you know that your fingerprint is unique? There is nobody else in the world who has the same pattern of ridges and swirls that you have on your finger. But that's not the only thing that makes you special. Nobody else has the same smile as you. Nobody else has the same voice as you. Nobody else walks the way you walk.

You are also unique on the inside. Nobody else has the same personality as you. Nobody else has the same collection of opinions, moods, thoughts and feelings. Nobody else sees the world quite like you do.

Being different is wonderful.

But sometimes being different can cause problems.

Peter and Thomas had very different personalities. They both wished the other would be just like them, but they seemed to be opposites in everything.

Peter was always late. Thomas was always early.

Peter liked to take risks. Thomas always played it safe.

Peter liked noise. Thomas wanted quiet.

Whenever Peter opened a window for fresh air, Thomas always closed it again because Thomas didn't like draughts.

And whenever Thomas wanted to go to bed early, Peter had invited all the neighbours round for a party.

Hardly a day – or night – went by when Peter and Thomas didn't disagree on something. The disagreements turned to

 arguments and the arguments turned to fights. Sometimes those fights got so bad that both of them ended up with bumps and bruises and cuts and scars.

The only thing Thomas and Peter ever agreed on was that Jesus was incredible. Neither of them had met anyone quite like him before. He helped people who were hungry, he welcomed those who were left out and he gave hope to people who otherwise had no hope. Thomas and Peter believed that one day he would be King. So they both left their jobs and their homes and joined Team Jesus.

'One day,' Peter would say, 'there's going to be an almighty battle and Team Jesus will overthrow those wretched Romans with swords and riots. Then Jesus will be King and we'll be famous.'

'I doubt that,' Thomas would reply. 'One day Jesus will give one of his amazing speeches and all the Italian invaders will realise they have to join our team. Then Jesus will be King and we'll be rich.'

Peter disagreed with Thomas, and Thomas argued with Peter. Both were convinced they were right.

Both were completely wrong.

After travelling all over the country for three years Team

Jesus finally arrived in the capital city for the
big showdown. Jesus would soon be King.

Peter bought himself a new sword.

Thomas bought himself a new wallet.

But there was no battle. Even when Jesus
was arrested, he refused to fight back.

And there was no speech. Even when Jesus was put on trial,
he didn't answer back.

Peter and Thomas were both very confused.

Even when Jesus heard his death sentence, even when he
was hung on a wooden cross, even when the crowd gathered
to laugh at him as he died, even when he took his last breath
– still Jesus did not start a riot, or deliver a last-minute earth-
shattering sermon.

'But I thought Jesus was the Messiah, the Son of the Living
God,' Peter shrugged. 'Now I don't know who he is.'

Thomas checked nobody was listening. He expected to be
arrested any minute. 'I thought Jesus was
the way, the truth and the life. Now he's
dead, and soon we will be too.'

Peter and Thomas didn't have time to argue – they had to go and hide with the rest of Team Jesus. They found a small room at the top of a house and locked themselves in. They all sat there feeling sad and angry that someone they loved very much had died. They felt upset and disappointed that all their hopes had been dashed. But more than anything they were terrified.

'I'm too young to die!'

'My sister won't cope without me!'

'Crucifixion looks so painful.'

'I'm going to miss the family get-together.'

'What was the point of my life?'

Neither Thomas nor Peter nor anyone else in the room got a wink of sleep all night. Or the next night. Or the night after that. For 72 hours straight they sat there getting more and more tired and hungry and scared.

Eventually they fell silent,
waiting for someone to knock on
the door, barge in and drag them
away to their own funeral.

Sure enough there was a knock
on the door. It started off soft and got
louder and louder.

Hearts leapt out of chests.

Lives flashed before eyes.

Bodies curled up in fright.

'It's only me!' came a soft voice through the keyhole.

'It's Mary!' Peter said, sitting up. 'Quick, let her in! Maybe she's brought us some food.'

But Thomas was suspicious. 'It's a trap! Don't let her in. Maybe it's

someone pretending to be Mary. They've probably brought the soldiers.'

'We're in here!' Peter called out.

'Oh no we're not!' said Thomas.

While Peter and Thomas argued, one of their friends unlocked the door. In came Mary with a big grin on her face. She was out of breath as though she'd been running, although she was still wearing her black funeral clothes. She was empty-handed and alone.

'You see!' Thomas shouted in Peter's face. 'No food!'

'You see!' Peter yelled at the same time. 'No soldiers!'

Mary was so excited she could hardly speak. It came

out rather
muddled, but
eventually she
managed to explain
that she had got up early,
visited Jesus' grave – which
was strangely open and empty – and
almost bumped into the gardener, who turned
out not to be the gardener. 'You'll never believe it – the
gardener was *Jesus*. He is back from the dead!'

'You're right,' said Thomas. 'I don't believe it.'

For once Peter agreed.

Not one person in the room believed Mary.
They thought she must have been confused.
She probably just imagined him. She
couldn't see straight with all the
crying. They all agreed that Mary
needed to go straight home to
have a lie down.

'I can't believe she visited the grave,' Peter said, as he locked the door behind her. 'She could have been arrested and killed.'

'I can't believe she visited *us*,' Thomas said. '*We* could have been arrested and killed.'

Peter and Thomas and the rest of the team squabbled together for a couple of hours, becoming more and more miserable.

Mary had reminded them how much they missed Jesus. He always kept them safe. He always helped them not to worry or argue. And he always made sure they had food to eat.

Eventually the miserable and hungry group decided that one of them had to risk his life to get some food for everyone. As Thomas was the only one who had any money, he was quickly voted the one for the job.

As soon as it began to get dark, he carefully unlocked the door and locked it behind him. He crept down the stairwell holding the key tightly in his hand, and darted off into the shadows. His heart was beating so fast he thought it might explode, but he did it! He found a little place that was still open, picked up some supplies, paid for them without being recognised, and headed back to what he very much hoped would be a bit of a hero's welcome.

When he unlocked the door again, the hungry, arguing, miserable bunch he had left behind had disappeared. Instead he found his friends sitting there with huge smiles on their faces. They were chattering and laughing and hugging one another.

They weren't interested in the food one bit.

'You'll never believe it, Thomas!' they all announced at once. 'It's a miracle! Jesus is alive! He was right here!'

'You're right!' Thomas said quickly. 'I don't believe it.'

Peter, who was doing a little dance in the middle of the room, turned to face Thomas. 'You should have been here! At first I thought he was a ghost. But it really was our Jesus, alive and well. I even saw the scars on his hands where the nails had been. We have to go and tell the world!'

'This is madness!' Thomas said, folding his arms and looking suspiciously at everyone. 'I know the door was locked, because I had the key. If you're trying to play a joke on me it's not funny. And if you're not, well that's not funny either. Eat the food and maybe you'll feel better.'

'Don't you trust us?' Peter said with a laugh. 'Would we make something like this up? It's a miracle none of us expected – although the more I think about it, the more it makes sense. Didn't Jesus even tell us this would happen?'

'It doesn't make sense at all,' Thomas argued. 'You say Jesus wasn't a ghost, but you also say he didn't need to open the door. You say he was alive and well, but you also say his hands had scars from being crucified to death. You say you're going to go and tell the world, but here you all are still hiding in this room.'

Thomas was beginning to feel annoyed. He would have stormed off, but he was too scared to leave. Instead he slumped down in the corner on his own and helped himself to the biggest sandwich. Who – or what – had they really seen? Why were they all so suddenly cheerful?

As Thomas chewed he mumbled to himself, 'If I'd been here, I would have asked more questions. I would have double-checked the facts. I would have demanded to see where the soldier put his sword in Jesus' side. I would have touched the scars.'

Thomas looked at his own scars and ran his
fingers over the shiny bumps and ridges. There
was the huge scar on his arm that he'd got
when he was younger from running
too fast down a rocky slope after
he'd been told to slow down. He
remembered the worried face of
his mum as she'd put ointment on
him while pretending to be cross.
He remembered her singing by his
bed when he couldn't sleep.

There was another scar on his foot where he'd burned
himself when he'd once helped Jesus cook fish on the fire.
And there were several other small scars that he'd mainly
got from various scrapes with Peter.

Each of the silvery puckered marks made him wince as he remembered the pain.

A week went by and Peter was still trying to persuade trying to persuade Thomas to believe him.

'Don't forget Mary saw him too!' he tried.

'Nobody would take a woman's opinion seriously in a Roman court of law,' Thomas said. 'You need to give me some facts.'

'What about that open and empty grave?'

'I'd have to see it for myself,' Thomas said.

Peter scratched his head. 'What about the scars?'

As far as Thomas was concerned, the scars supported his line of argument. They had all seen Jesus die – his lungs had collapsed, his heart had stopped beating, and blood had poured down from his head and his side. What sort of strange resurrection was it if Jesus' heart and lungs and side were suddenly miraculously working again – but his skin was still scarred?

There was nothing Peter could say to convince Thomas that Jesus was alive. And there was nothing Thomas could say to convince Peter not to go out and tell the world.

'It's a crazy story – nobody will believe you.'

'Of course they will!' Peter said. 'Look around you. Whoever designed this world we live in is surely able to raise a man from the dead. People

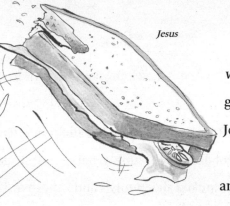

Jesus

will flock to hear our good news and accept Jesus as King.'

'Unless they don't and they decide to kill you.' Secretly Thomas really didn't want Peter to be killed too.

'If they kill me,' Peter said, 'I'll get to go to Jesus' kingdom and be with him there.'

'Unless Jesus really is dead – which he _is_.'

'Which he _was_ – and now he's alive.'

Thomas and Peter argued and argued. They stood closer and closer, and their voices got louder and louder. Soon they were pushing and insulting each other too.

'You always think you're right, Fish-face!' said Thomas grabbing the sandwich from Peter's hand and launching it across the room.

'Only when you're wrong, Diddy-chops!' said Peter grabbing Thomas' waist and turning him upside down.

The boys were so busy arguing they nearly didn't notice there was somebody else in the room.

Thomas spotted him first. His jaw dropped down. His heart missed a beat.

'Jesus?!' he spluttered. And the room fell silent.

'Peace be with you!' Jesus said smiling.

Thomas and Peter looked sheepishly at one another. The thing about Jesus was that his timing was always perfect.

'So Thomas,' Jesus continued and held out his hands towards him, 'here are my scars for you to feel.

Reach out your hand and put it into my side.'

'My Lord ... My God ...'

Thomas didn't know what else to say. Jesus was back! His Jesus! He'd come back just for Thomas, even though Thomas had been so suspicious and rude. Now Thomas had no doubt who Jesus was.

A few weeks later and Peter and Thomas were arguing again.

'Yes, but I saw him first,' Peter said smugly as he threw a couple of fish on the barbecue.

'Yes, but he came back especially for me,' Thomas replied as he poked the flaming logs.

'Yes, but that's because you doubted that his scars were real.'

'Yes, but ...'

Thomas stopped himself. He knew that Jesus' scars meant more to him than he could ever explain. They were not only proof of the resurrection, and proof of God's undying love for all people everywhere, but proof that Jesus understood him. His scars and Jesus' scars had become part of the same story. That story began in brokenness and pain and ended in forgiveness and joy.

That story couldn't stay trapped in a grave or locked behind a door. That story would go out and face the difficulties and dangers of the world because there was a new King on the throne.

Peter and Thomas prepared the meal together for all the hundreds of people who had joined them in accepting the good news that Jesus was Lord and King. And Thomas hummed a song to himself. It was the one his mum had sung to him all those years ago. Now he finally understood what the words meant.

'Who would have believed it?
Seen the Lord's hand in it?
The punishment on him brought us peace
And by his wounds we are healed.'

Just like our fingerprints, our scars are unique to each of us. Whatever difficulties and pain they remind us of, they can also help us to remember that God loves us so much that he sent Jesus to die so we can have eternal life. You can read Thomas' story in John 20. The song is from Isaiah 53.

JOE'S STORY

This is Joe. His brain is wired differently to most people's and he often has trouble understanding the world around him. Sometimes other people have trouble understanding him and the world he lives in too.

They might not understand why he covers his ears when he's scared, or why he can't go into school unless he's the first in the line, or why he looks away when he's trying to work out how to answer a question.

They often don't realise that changes in routine make him feel like he's drowning and that a small graze on his knee feels like the worst pain ever. Joe has experienced all sorts of difficulties in his life and yet he always tries to be brave and strong and kind. That makes him a hero in our eyes and we couldn't feel more proud that he is part of our family.

I would love to introduce Joe to Paul. Paul is a hero of the Bible and did many amazing things for God even though life wasn't always easy for him either.

207

PAUL

THE TALE OF THE PRISONER WHO HAD A BAD SIDE

The wind howled.

The sea roared.

The ship lurched.

And the sword glistened.

'Don't even think about trying to escape!' the soldier
threatened nervously, pointing a razor-sharp blade right
between his prisoners' eyes.

One prisoner laughed. There was literally nowhere to
escape to. The grey swelling ocean stretched for miles in every
direction around him.

The soldier squinted suspiciously. 'For all I know you could
be planning to swim to safety, prisoner 161.'

'Please, Julius, just call me Paul. And have you seen those

huge waves? Do you know how freezing cold that water is? Even if I could swim, which I can't, home is hundreds, maybe thousands, of miles away! It would be an impossible plan.'

Paul was laughing so much his side hurt. They were about to spend several weeks on board the Pride of Alexandria together, which he knew would be more of a hardship for the nervous-looking soldier than for him.

'So you're stuck with me, Julius,' he said. 'And, in case you've forgotten, there's a trial waiting for me in Rome and I *do not* want to miss it.'

Now it was the soldier's turn to laugh. 'You *want* to stand trial? For crimes against the empire?! Are you mad? You know that in Rome they feed convicts to the lions, right?!'

'Soldiers who let their prisoners escape also get fed to the lions,' Paul said, watching Julius squirm behind the hilt of his sword. 'But don't worry, you can sit back and enjoy the cruise. I'm not going anywhere.'

Paul had felt God telling him to go to Rome to spread the good news about Jesus being resurrected from the dead. But he never imagined he would be travelling on the very latest in luxury sail craft. Compared to the last boat he'd been on, a battered little old sea ferry that should have been turned into firewood years ago, this 1000-tonne giant gleaming with brand new varnish and shiny paint was like something from the future.

'The *Pride of Alexandria* is truly an incredible feat of engineering!' Paul said to his friend Doctor Luke, as they sat together below deck. 'Did you know it's equipped with the very latest in navigation systems, has a reinforced hull, and all the safety features you could imagine? It can carry an amazing 400 tonnes of cargo as well as 276 people. And you should take a look at the anchors! They are immense!'

'How can you possibly be admiring a boat at a time like this?' Doctor Luke replied. 'Everyone in Jerusalem wants you dead and even the government in Rome knows about it. I hear the lions are being starved ready to eat you for dinner! And if that wasn't bad enough I'm pretty sure a storm is coming and none of us can swim.'

'I've been through worse,' Paul replied with a laugh.

It was true. Paul had survived more terrifying experiences than most of us put together. The plot of his life was like all the action movies you've ever seen rolled into one.

He'd been beaten with a rod by Roman soldiers not just once but three times.

He'd been chained to a post and faced with a torturous whipping not just once but five times.

He'd been beaten up and left for dead in the dust by the side of the road not just once but so many times he'd lost count.

He'd once even faced execution by stoning – and still somehow survived.

That wasn't all.

He'd been robbed.

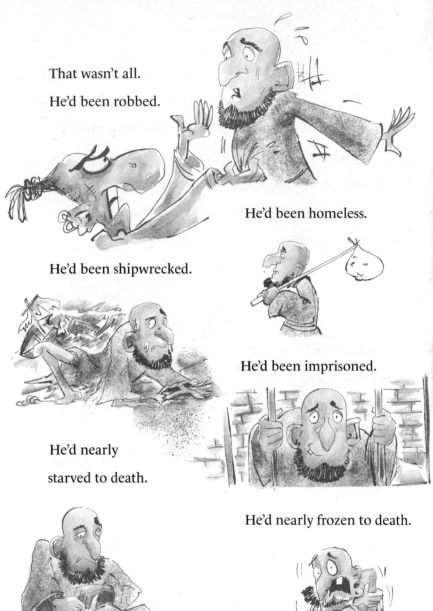

He'd been homeless.

He'd been shipwrecked.

He'd been imprisoned.

He'd nearly
starved to death.

He'd nearly frozen to death.

'But God protected me every time, Luke!' Paul said. 'So I'm not going to be scared of a few hungry lions.'

'I wish I wasn't scared of those lions,' Doctor Luke replied.

That night Paul woke up in agony. A terrible pain was shooting down his side, and sweat poured off his face. He could hardly move. The tossing and turning of the ship in the waves made it worse.

Doctor Luke came rushing in but none of his treatments seemed  to help. Paul continued to cry out in pain as the wind and the rain battered the boat.

'Maybe this is just my time to die, Luke,' Paul said. 'I'm not afraid. I only wish it didn't hurt so much.'

'Maybe your God wants you dead as much as I do,' Julius jeered. He picked himself and his sword up off the floor after a particularly violent wave had hit the ship side on. 'Then there'd be one less crazy prisoner for me to be responsible for in this terrible storm.'

'All hands on deck!' It was the captain. Things must have got desperate.

Paul had no choice. With help from Doctor Luke and Julius he managed to get up the stairs into the open air where the storm had turned into a hurricane. It was chaos. The mast had snapped in two. The navigation system had gone haywire. The soaking wet crew were desperately throwing tables and chairs and cargo over the side of the ship to lighten the load.

But even though one of the sea anchors had been dropped, the storm was still dragging the boat along. They were now so far off course the captain didn't know which way to steer.

Paul was in too much pain to be of any help. So he prayed. He prayed that the storm would stop and he prayed the ship would be saved and he prayed his side would be healed.

'I don't think your God can hear you above the thunder and roaring wind!' Julius shouted. 'Faith is no good in times like this.'

The next day things were no better. Paul was still in agony, the storm was still raging, the ship still looked tired and beaten. Now even the first-class passengers were helping to throw the cargo overboard.

Paul prayed again that the storm would stop and the ship would be saved and his side would be healed.

'Your God doesn't care about you,' Julius sneered as the storm got even worse. 'He's just a figment of your imagination.'

On the third day, all 276 people on board were more miserable, hungry, tired and scared than they had ever been. They were covered in bruises from being thrown around inside the boat by the huge waves. There was nothing left to hurl overboard. They were all doomed. Paul prayed for the third time. He prayed the storm would stop and the ship would be saved and his side would be healed.

'I know God can stop storms,' Paul said to Luke. 'He's done it before. And I know God can heal people. I've seen him raise people from the dead with my own eyes. What's going on? Why won't he help me now?'

It's not easy when people say 'No' to us, especially when we really need help. Paul was getting the distinct feeling that God was saying 'No' to him.

The storm got stronger hour by hour. The ship was falling apart plank by plank. And Paul's side hurt so much he couldn't even stand up straight.

As darkness fell on the *7th* night, the *10th* night, the *14th* night, everyone on board had given up all hope. They felt as though they'd been imprisoned on an eternal rollercoaster at a funfair that was not at all fun and not at all fair. Using any scraps of rope or clothing they could salvage, they tied themselves to the side of the ship and lay down. If they were lucky perhaps they would fall asleep and not feel themselves sink beneath the waves.

Paul looked around at the 275 desperate souls and wished there was something he could do besides pray. The wind carried on howling. The boat was buffeted left then right, almost sinking with each wave that hit.

With the next flash of lightning that lit up the night sky Paul saw something unexpected on the deck. It looked like someone walking around, but surely that was impossible. Nobody could stand up on this   lurching, lumbering excuse for a ship.

But with the next flash, Paul saw him again. He quickly threw him a rope but the man shook his head.

'Thank you but I don't need it. I've just come to deliver a message.'

'A message?' Paul said, surprised. 'At a time like this? But … but … who are you? And how did you get here?'

The man smiled. 'I'm a messenger – an angel if you like. God sent me.'

Paul was about to laugh. Then he suddenly remembered another journey he'd been on when lightning had flashed and God had appeared to him with a message. It was a long time ago, but it had changed his life, and stopped many people from dying needlessly.

'What did you wake me up for?' Julius snapped, leaping at Paul's throat. 'Why can't you let me die in peace? I've had just about enough of you.'

The Roman soldier pulled out his sword and lifted it high. The metal reflected the daylight that was creeping over the horizon. One swing and Paul's head would be removed from his body before breakfast time.

'Wait! You're *not* going to die!' Paul called out. 'And neither am I. God told me.'

'God told you?! Oh really?! And what else did he say? That tomorrow we'll all be sitting on an island sipping cocktails with the locals in the sunshine while our clothes dry off around a warm fire?'

'What exactly did the messenger say?' Doctor Luke asked, positioning himself carefully between his friend and the sarcastic soldier with his sharp sword.

By now all the passengers were listening. Half of them looked curious. The other half looked as though they'd have been very happy to help throw Paul's body – and head – overboard.

'Well,' Paul said, 'first the angel said that God was not going to stop the storm, like I prayed, but that God would bring us *through* the storm. Secondly he said God wasn't going to save the ship, like I prayed, but would save everyone on board.'

There was a murmur in the crowd. Could this be true? Had God seen their plight? Was he stronger than the storm?

'Didn't you also ask God for a third thing?' Luke whispered.

Paul sighed. 'God's not going to heal my side, Luke, but he will help me. That's good enough for me.'

'Why would your God talk to you?' Julius butted back in. 'You're just a prisoner, no better than the rest of us. You can't even stand up straight. Nobody is going to believe that we'll survive this storm when we're miles from anywhere and this boat is about to sink to the bottom of the deep, deep ocean!'

Suddenly the captain shouted: 'Land ahoy!'

Everyone looked up. Everyone gasped. Then everyone cheered. Perhaps Paul was right after all!

As they got closer they saw that the land that was ahoy was a treacherous pile of rocks. The cheers turned to wails. This was worse than a storm. They were about to be dashed to pieces.

The captain ran around in circles not knowing what to do and everyone else began to panic too.

Only Paul remained calm. 'Stop worrying. Nobody will die!' he shouted.

'*Everybody* will die!' Julius yelled back between sobs. 'Can't you see those rocks?

Your God can't save us now.'

Just as the ship was about to career into the rocks, there was a bump and it stopped dead in its tracks. The huge hull had hit a sandbank. The bad news was that the boat was letting in water through the hole. The good news was that it meant land was close by.

'If we exit starboard we can follow the sandbank and swim to safety,' the captain announced. 'It's dangerous but not impossible.'

Everyone rushed to untie their ropes and risk the swim in the freezing cold water. Nobody wanted to go down with the sinking ship.

Before they dived in, the captain had one last instruction.

'Err... In the event of an

emergency landing such as
this is, I am ordered to first execute
all prisoners on board to prevent
them escaping.'

The captain looked at Julius.

Julius looked at Paul.

Paul looked at Luke.

Luke looked at all the other prisoners.

The other prisoners looked at the sharp sword.

'I'm sorry,' Julius replied after a long pause. 'I can't follow
your order, Captain. I'm beginning to think that
Paul's God may have saved our lives after all.'

That night, Julius, Paul, the captain and the other 273 crew and passengers of the once seaworthy *Pride of Alexandria* huddled together on a beach trying to get warm and dry. The residents of the island, who had all turned up to help the half-drowned refugees, were soon offering them food and dry clothes.

'How is your painful side?' Luke asked Paul when he'd checked that nobody else needed medical attention.

'It's bad,' Paul said, wincing a little, 'but it's also good. It makes me trust in God's power, which is stronger than the strongest storm.'

'And the hungriest lion?'

'Absolutely!' Paul said.

Paul eventually got to Rome, and he wasn't eaten by lions. But he was a prisoner for many years, and the pain, or 'thorn in his side', never went away. None of that stopped him being part of God's great adventure. Despite everything, maybe because of it, he helped millions of people to know the power of God even in the most difficult of circumstances. You can read this story in Acts 27 and 28 and 2 Corinthians 11.

ABOUT THE AUTHORS

Krish works with government, churches and communities to support children who go through difficult times. He and his wife Miriam have been foster carers for 16 years and currently live with six children, an auntie, a friend, a cat and a rabbit. Krish and Miriam love not only writing books and stories for children but hearing and reading inspirational stories of children from around the world.

ABOUT THE ILLUSTRATOR

Andy S. Gray has been drawing for as long as he can remember. He's also a DJ, producer, speaker, magician, and even a Church of England minister. He's worked professionally with children and young people for over 30 years in schools and churches. Sometimes he gets bored. He is proud to be autistic and encourages people to embrace their uniqueness and live life to the full.

ACKNOWLEGEMENTS

One huge heartfelt thank you goes out to all the amazing children in our life. You have inspired us to write these tales and let them loose into the world so that children just like you can be encouraged. We hope you enjoy spotting the telltale signs of your stories in the pages of this book.

Another huge heartfelt thank you goes out to all the enthusiastic children who read our first *Whistlestop Tales* book and asked for more. We heard you, and sincerely hope you love these ones too.

Our third huge heartfelt thank you goes out to the wonderful Andy Gray, Ruth Roff, Jessica Lacey, Alexa Tewkesbury, Natalie Chen, Emily Short, Linda DeAngelis and the team at Hodder Faith Young Explorers, and Kay Morgan-Gurr and Revd Kate Bottley. We are so grateful to you for your encouragement and support. Thank you for generously spending long hours illustrating and editing, reading and re-reading, promoting and endorsing, and much more to steer the project forward.

Hodder & Stoughton is the UK's
leading Christian publisher with
a wide range of books from the
bestselling authors in the UK and
around the world. Having published
Bibles and Christian books for
more than 150 years, Hodder &
Stoughton are delighted to launch
Hodder Faith Young Explorers – a
list of books for children.

Join us on this new adventure!